Witty Banter

The Art & Science of Being Charismatic, Clever, and Likeable

By: Discover Press

Table of Contents

Part One

I saw her from across the room. She was talking to a group of people, creating colorful starbursts with her hands, and making silly faces. I couldn't hear what she was saying, but I could see how happy she seemed to make the people around her. They were utterly enthralled by whatever she was describing. Then without warning, the entire group erupted in a fit of laughter, and she became magic.

I've often wondered how someone could become the life of the party. Are you born with such talents, or can they be learned? Is there a class I could take? A conversational mentor, if you will? Alas, there is no college for wallflowers, but fear not. Since that very night, I have worked tirelessly to develop a foolproof plan to get you out of your corner cocoon so you can emerge as the social butterfly you were always meant to be.

In this book, I will walk you through the process of becoming charismatic, clever, and likable. If you are reading this book, you must have an inner butterfly that flutters around inside your chest, just waiting to spread its beautiful wings. While you are comfortable in the crowd, you long to be an entertaining conversationalist like the enchanted woman I saw that night. Natural charisma isn't something you can buy, sell, or trade. Still, it is something you can unearth through an intricate system of self-discovery.

I have developed, mastered, and instructed this technique online and at multiple college lecture tours throughout the last 20 years. Today I share my "The Second Big Bang" method with you. In any instance of change, you must define long-term goals and then create a comprehensive description and illustration of how and why this particular change must occur. Normally, when a person wishes to change, they assume it begins once you make the proclamation for change. But in reality, it begins with initiative. Saying you will change isn't the same as changing. That's just a game your mind likes to play with you.

Instead of playing chess with your brain, let's play hide-and-go-seek with your subconscious. The first rule of thumb in this game we call life, is to realize you absolutely cannot win if you never roll the dice. So, let's get to it, shall we?

It all starts with getting your feet wet, so step out of the shadows and into the conversational current.

Chapter 1:
The Conversational Current

"Sometimes, in the wave of change, we find our true direction."

— Unknown

A conversation is nothing more than a series of questions and answers. The understanding of making the recipient feel comfortable and entertained, is the key to creating a steady flow by guiding the conversation. When you feel in control of the narrative, you can create an engaging experience.

One common mistake made in conversations is confidence or lack thereof. To be more confident when speaking to someone instead of fighting against nervousness, accept it. Nervousness is no different than feeling hungry or excited. Understanding that being anxious isn't dangerous makes us "less afraid of feeling afraid." This isn't a complicated mind trick in any way. It's a simple process of bringing your focus back to the conversation when you end up in your head.

Essentially, the idea behind a conversational current is to mimic an actual current by collecting oneself and allowing the conversation to find a rhythm that carries both parties back and forth. Although you will find no matter how hard you try, the conversation falls flat in some cases. In instances such as these, do not take responsibility for any awkward silences. Try not to run away inside your head and overanalyze the situation. Like you, the other person is also trying to come up with something to say. They may even think you are waiting for them to come up with a new topic or clever antidote; being aware of this may help take some of the pressure off.

Have you ever found yourself in a conversation with someone who replies with one word? It can seem like a world of "K's" and "I know, right?" You might feel as if you are living in a 3D version of Google Meets. There is actually a term for these types of conversationalists, if you can even call them that. They are called "one-word wonders" and can be the bane of any party's existence. I've noticed throughout my days in the "party scene", that these types of people are not only aloof and positively irritating, but they are also quite rude. One-liners are great when you're a comic, but less so when you try to create an invariable exchange. I tend to picture these types of people as rocks. What I mean by that is I picture tossing them into a river and watching them drown. I bet they come up with some exciting topics after a near-death experience.

Me: "Hey Tom, I heard you drowned." Tom: "Yeah."

Oh my god.

I would advise you to discover these types of people as soon as you arrive. You can use them as practice for the other normal human beings you will be engaging with throughout the night. While it can be daunting, the first step in creating a flow of conversation that entices the attention of the other partygoers is a mutually interesting topic. In my extensive research, I noticed one tip stood out the most.

Familiarize yourself with open-ended conversation starters. These are questions or topics that cannot be answered with a simple "yes" or "no." They are intended to be thought-provoking and require intelligent feedback. Tom would not be a good respondent to present these to, because of his pea-sized brain. But don't be discouraged; simply move on to another guest, or better yet, a group of guests. When entering a conversation already in progress, ask yourself:

Do I comprehend the subject enough to weigh in? What can I add to the conversation? Is there an opening for a quippy side note? Is there a chance I could make them laugh?

If the conversation is a serious one, such as politics, failed love lives (this is usually reserved for the end of the party when a group of sobbing girls is semi-passed out around the pool screaming the lyrics to Lizzo's *Cuz I Love You* album), or workplace stresses, it can result in negativity soaking up your brilliant atmosphere. If the conversation is light and airy, make your move. For example, if the conversation is "If you had intro music, what song would it be and why?" Conversations like this are fantastic if you can execute them correctly. When one person has the floor, they feel pragmatic and special. If you are a wallflower, you could miss out on getting to know your peers. Join these conversations; they are a great way to introduce yourself without having a full-blown conversation with anyone in particular.

The best advice I have ever received was from a close friend who happens to be a comedian. He said "If there is a chance to be funny, take it; crowds gravitate toward funny people." So, my answer to this question would be "White and Nerdy" by Weird Al Yankovic. Why? Because I literally edit Wikipedia pages for fun, was captain of a chess club, and how can you deny the sweet beats of "Riding" by Chamillionaire and Krayzie Bone. Google it; you will not be disappointed. Nine times out of ten, the crowd would erupt in laughter, making me the most interesting person at the party, even if it is for only a brief second. What you will find is after the conversation fizzles, people will now feel comfortable approaching you, and so begins the venture to become the life of the party, one thoughtful discussion at a time.

Chapter 2: From Boring to Bonding

"Charm was a scheme for making strangers like and trust a person immediately, no matter what the charmer had in mind."
— Kurt Vonnegut

I can't think of social encounters without thinking of the pleasure of a great conversation. I have been blessed throughout the years with a wide range of friends with varying careers, each unique in their own way. What makes all of these humans similar is their unique ability to carry on a rich and vivid dialogue from start to finish.

Imagine genuinely connecting with someone in such a way that time seems to stand still, the sound of the restaurant fades to a soft hum, and you realize you are so proud and thankful to be a part of such an intelligent group of people that makes you feel so alive. Suppose you have never been a part of a discussion circle or an exhilarating debate leaving you feeling accomplished and smarter by the end of dinner. In that case, I suggest you widen your circle of friends. Invite work colleagues that you find exciting or visit online forums for discussion dinners. You will find plenty of people that welcome new ideas and points of view.

My version of hell would have to be endless small talk and awkward silences. As I have mentioned before, I like to discover these types of draining conversationalists at the very beginning of the party or conference. Surreptitious discourse is just not in my wheelhouse. It leaves me feeling like I've just finished jackhammering concrete for an hour.

While you may already have a knack for carrying conversations on your back like a word mule, I have a little crowdsourced wisdom for becoming better at small talk if you just cannot avoid these monotony missiles.

1. Ask open-ended questions: Let's face it, one-word answers can make you want to punch the teenager out of some adults. Instead, let's think of a more civilized solution. When asking a small-talky question, make sure to phrase it in a way that prompts the use of detail.

Example: "Hello, are you here with your family?" This is a question that will most certainly get a one-word answer, "yes" or "no." To avoid being left with the bag, ask this, "What brings you here tonight?" This promotes detail, and nine times out of ten, this will be a chance for the other person to quickly share why they came. This leads to casual conversation with a natural back and forth dialogue, maybe even introducing new subjects.

2. Gamify for your own amusement: Meaning elevate your excitement for whatever you are saying and your reactions to whatever they say. If you act bored, the conversational tone will be boring, and no one wants to talk to boring people. If you are having a great time, others will enjoy talking to you.

Example: "Hello! Wow, nice shirt! Where did you get it? I absolutely love that color! So, what brings you here tonight?" You see how I went in with a candid approach, complimenting the woman's shirt, and asking a question that prompted detail. And hopefully leaving her with a smile.

3. Be interesting: This is as simple as it gets, folks! Draw attention to yourself with your wardrobe or laughter. This creates a comfortable demeanor. After all, the first principle of good conversation is to be genuinely interested in your discourse counterpart & vice versa. Small talk is only as small as your contribution to the conversational current. Also, expand your understanding of anecdotes and banter. This will undoubtedly make you more interesting across the board.

Chapter 3: Absolutely No Absolutes

"You don't win a debate by suppressing discussion; you win it with a better argument."

— Frank Sonnenberg

Absolutes are quantifiable words or statements that leave no room for debate. Words such as always or never, can come off as pompous and defensive. The last thing you want to be in a social situation is "The Know it All." We've all been subjected to this type of interaction at one point or another. The "Ugh, here comes Bob with his scientific babble; quick pretend like we are doing something, so he doesn't talk to us" plight is real. To avoid sounding like a self-promoting troll, try instead to use a structure to establish a healthy raconteur. Don't get me wrong, Bob is not necessarily a bad person. While Bob is clearly his biggest fan, what he may not realize is how off-putting his statements actually are.

The only thing that happens "always" is the rotation of the earth. Remember that when you are tempted to say "My mom is the <u>best</u> cook." or "This <u>always</u> happens to me." You cannot say with absolute certainty that there is no one else in the world who can make your mother's famous brisket. This opens up the conversation to comparisons and usually ends with someone getting their feelings hurt. By slightly changing your banter, you will retain a sense of credibility and seem less matter-of-fact and more rational.

I know this one is a hard pill to swallow. You're probably replaying several conversations in your head right now. That one time when you declared "Trader Joe's is the best store ever!" then someone else said "Whole Foods is and always will be better than Trader Joe's." While on the surface, it might sound like a healthy debate. The reality is that it's an uncreative approach and reduces the continuance of conversation.

When navigating a conversation route about your favorite store, try using "consistently" in place of "always" and instead of "best" say "excellent." Let's try it. "Trader Joe's is consistently stocked and has excellent customer service!" This leaves plenty of space for opinions. "That's awesome, but have you been to Whole Foods? They have an immaculate vegan section!" See how that simple fix allows the chat to flourish, leaving plenty of room for other opinions to follow. Remember, a great conversation can go back and forth. If you speak in absolutes, your fellow participants could peg you as "all or nothing" or the worst possible tag ever "The Opinionated One."

Careful to avoid opinions for fear of being tagged "opinionated." Being pragmatic isn't a derogatory personality trait. It means you are passionate about what it is you believe in or are talking about. What gets you labeled opinionated isn't the assertiveness of your beliefs; it's the bullheadedness and the constant need to draw a line in the sand. Being opinionated can be endearing as long as you watch your tone and delivery.

Choose to be inspiring and less preachy when discussing your point of view, and it will serve you well.

While steering clear of cognitive distortions, these are not objective interpretations of what you've experienced, and be aware of unconscious interjection. This means speaking out of turn or the classic blurting out of needless or offensive judgments. A good rule of thumb in these types of situations is simply stopping, thinking, and reacting. While this might sound elementary, it is a lot harder than it seems. Your tone and delivery shape the way people respond to you. A loudmouth influencer with a knack for inciting drama is acceptable in contentious TV shows or controversial whale hunting documentaries.

When I attended a conference on racial biases and their effect on the subconscious, I remember being blown away by the simplistic explanation of something called "Programming." While I am not new to the idea of reprogramming your brain (it's kind of what I do), I was intrigued by the theory of generational programming.

Generational programming is essentially a series of faiths and belief systems passed down through generations. We all know the most common perspectives are normally passed down from great grandparents to their children and so on. Some of them are religion, values, and social concepts. But this theory suggests that intentionally or even unintentionally, core beliefs are passed down without you ever knowing where these beliefs stemmed from.

The generational study is essential, helping families sift through and understand how their families have evolved over a series of time. Take my family, for instance. I was raised in between two tall hills called a "holler." My family would rarely leave our holler; only for grocery shopping or school and sometimes the occasional vacation. But more often than not, we lived and congregated between those two huge hills.

Have you ever heard of the term "Negative Nancy" or "Brazen Brittney"? These two personalities are known for speaking louder than anyone else in the house. They are easily the most annoying people at any engagement. No one can understand why someone would even invite them. To speak out of turn or blurt out assumptions is a great way to get your personality in quotations. To break the habit of consistently talking too much, practice the hold your tongue technique. You guessed it—it is the process is holding your tongue. When you close your mouth, you reduce the likelihood of offending the person speaking exponentially. Many of your peers will have different opinions than you. Instead of immediately releasing your point of view, ask yourself four questions.

1. Is it true?
2. Is it constructive?
3. Is it inspiring?
4. Is it kind?

Knowing when to speak is just as important as what you say. When speaking on a subject that is obtuse in nature, try not to add any more nonsensical information. Instead, try adding a bit of humor to the dull conversation. Choose peace over persecution; use this as a way to showcase your social graces. If the conversation is about the weather, tell them about the funny essay you wrote on how you solved the timeless riddle of Mother Nature's consistent rage.

"The reason for all the floods, fires, and earthquakes is because Mother Nature, while in her fourth trimester, specifically asked Father Time to bring her home Rocky Road ice cream from the grocery. Regretfully, he got Chocolate Chip Cookie Dough instead. Because of Father Time's epic blunder, he now sleeps on the couch. Meanwhile, in Thailand, people are floating on couches due to Mother Nature's fluid mood swings. Talk about unnecessary roughness." More often than not, that one always kills and quickly creates a more lucent vibe in the room.

You see what I did there, right? I took a bland, uneventful discourse, likely to induce snoring, and made it absurdly charming. The follow-up conversations now have permission to be silly and less likely to bore the crap out of you. I have a rule at all parties I host. First—no talk of the weather. We can all see the rain, Donald, I don't need a play by play. And second—no talk of politics.

Politics. I don't need to tell you the importance of not blending friendships or first encounters with bias blocked listening skills. Blocked listening is where the phrase "in one ear and out the other" comes from. It is self-explanatory, really, meaning someone is not hearing your side of the argument or simply doesn't retain anything you've said because they deem it nonsense or incorrect. So, it is best to hold your tongue in these types of situations or walk away. Nothing good can come from a radical right-wing nd a far-left liberal debate.

These outlets (not to speak in absolutes) most always end in losing friendships or a general lack of respect for both parties for arguing about tax cuts and the 5th Amendment. Whenever I find myself in a political hailstorm, the end result is always somebody shouting "You wanna take this outside?" Really, guys, you are so hell-bent on proving your intelligence that you revert to caveman tactics? "Betty, open the door so Harold and Sam can lose all rational credibility. Also, lock the door behind them."

Be sensible people; not everything needs to be black and white. Watching your tone and thinking before you say something you cannot take back holds much weight when it comes to your reputation.

Chapter 4:
The Power of Persuasion

"The most important persuasion tool you have in your entire arsenal is integrity."

— Zig Ziglar

This system is largely misunderstood because of persuasion being compared to manipulation. While the two have similar properties, unlike manipulation, persuasion is intended to convince someone of something that may, in our opinion, genuinely benefit them, such as switching churches. Salesmen and women have been using this tactic since the first vacuum cleaner was invented. Try telling my mom she didn't need that set of encyclopedias she paid a grand for in '92. She would agree that the salesman did nothing but charismatically prove to her the need to advance her children's learning. Never mind the fact that they became nothing but a conversational piece at family get-togethers, ultimately becoming a huge inconvenience when it came to taking up space and a receptacle for dust.

Manipulation often hides behind persuasive techniques. Unlike persuasion, manipulation normally has underlying intent. Your manipulator isn't in it for your best interest but for their own agenda. For example, emotional manipulators might prey on weak or recently traumatized individuals. The easiest way to alert a schemer is to share too much too fast. When you first meet someone, there is a thin line between introducing yourself and revealing yourself. Careful to not cross it because the person standing in front of you may or may not use this information against you.

When it comes to creating a profile for yourself in a social situation, persuasion can assist in shaping the way people perceive you. When developing a model of who you are, make sure to include your talents. These will further your credibility. For instance, when someone asks you "What do you think your most interesting talent is?" The best answer is something you can prove right away. I'll illustrate it for you:

"Oh wow, there are so many." — This shows you are light and funny without you even having to address it. No one, and I repeat, no one wants to hear how funny you think you are. "I would have to say I'm flexible (go ahead insert that clever wink); I can do a triple backflip!" When you get the attention from the crowd and if there is adequate space to, prove it. It can create a silly "hold my beer" moment that will ensure your name is sprinkled over all of the water cooler conversations come Monday morning.

It is remarkably easy to persuade your peers into thinking you are fascinating if you have the chops to back it up. Even wallflowers have the ability to get in on this action. While on a business trip with other colleagues, most of them were fairly good conversationalists considering we didn't know one another very well. Amongst my new co-workers was a nervous-looking woman who barely spoke at all. This young woman was the full embodiment of your typical wallflower.

Halfway through the trip, we were all at dinner, and someone asked "So what does everyone do for fun?"

We went around the table explaining our hobbies; some of them were things like golf and collecting seashells and painting. Then it was Vanessa's turn. She stood up with a sense of confident pride and said "Stripping!" We all gasped as if we had just seen a celebrity; of course, I couldn't handle the shock and, for some reason, started slow clapping as if she had just blown me away with her performance. Of course, in this instance, we didn't ask her to prove it because her sheer transparency was enough.

Chapter 5: Are There Perks to Being a Wallflower?

"The only perspective is to really be there."

— Stephen Chbosky

We can all take a cue from Vanessa; she wasn't embarrassed by her hobby in any sense of the word. Why? Because she wasn't afraid to be different, and that takes more guts than you would think. In a world full of people trying to "fit in", Vanessa chose to stand out. While she may seem reserved on the surface, she isn't afraid to embrace what makes her happy.

We all know at least one wallflower. They typically stand back from the limelight when possible. These types of people do not like to be noticed. While intentionally becoming invisible isn't technically a bad thing, it does limit the chances of showing the world what you are made of. Wallflowers are the epitome of blending in. I mean, it's right there in the name. The name itself describes the eponymous plant that used to grow on the inside/outside of a home to hide cracks or gaps in stone walls. Wallflowers would literally stand as close to the walls as possible at balls and social gatherings rather than mingling.

In the olden days, these types of people were deemed socially awkward or suffered from mental issues such as anxiety, low self-esteem, or depression. Having a daughter who isn't just a wallflower, but quite literally a potted plant, I know this is as far from the truth as it gets. Around the age of 10, I noticed my daughter began pulling away at family events and birthday parties. I would always find her in a room no one was in reading a book or drawing, even at her own birthday party! Worried, I took her to the doctor, hoping it wasn't something more serious, and was met with laughter. Her doctor spoke with her alone, trying to weed out depression and anxiety. When they returned to the waiting room, they were in stitches. Confused, I asked "What's so funny?" Her doctor then sat down next to me and explained "What we have here is a classic case of misanthropy! I haven't actually seen this before in her age group." He said with a hearty chuckle. "Umm. Excuse me, miss-what?" I asked, growing annoyed with his humorous reaction. "Your daughter, put simply, doesn't like people. So, she avoids them at all costs. It's nothing to worry about; it should fade as she grows." My mouth dropped wide open, and everything began to make sense.

Since birth, my daughter has had this superior look in her eyes and even refused to talk to anyone besides her immediate family until she turned five years old. I'm not kidding when I tell you there were whispers throughout the family that my child might be mute. As laughable as that was, I knew very well that my child chose not to speak to them. Since then, I have just accepted the fact of her introverted-ness.

As the years passed and she entered school, almost immediately, I was brought in for a conference about her shyness and refusal to interact with her classmates. As worried as they were about her, I assured them that she would eventually come around. She did not. Now I know why. But don't worry yourself too much about my wallflower. She is older now and has, wait for it… three whole friends, and that is simply fine with her.

Have no fear, my little daisies. If you long to break free from the concrete, I have some sure-fire tips to get you unstuck and into the sunshine where you belong.

1. Be honest with yourself: Ask yourself, from where does your shyness stem? Is it a lack of confidence or a fear of judgment? If it is confidence, find a mirror and begin practicing social engagements. Pretend you are speaking to another guest while holding your head high; put some bass in your voice and conquer that fear one day at a time.

2. Be approachable: Hiding in the corner doesn't make you invisible. People can still see you. Avoiding eye contact is the quickest way to be deemed a serial killer. While practicing in the mirror or with friends, make sure to hold eye contact for at least 50% of the conversation. This allows the other party the ability to read you and trust you, meanwhile alleviating the chance of you murdering them in their sleep.

3. Don't take yourself so seriously: There is a common misconception surrounding parties or social gatherings. Nine times out of ten, the person you are conversing with is three sheets to the wind, meaning they are inebriated, and won't even remember you spoke. So, try out some of the things you've been practicing without fear or anxiety. I promise you

the party's more interesting when you are inside the crowd, rather than watching it.

So, get out there and mingle, and remember while you may be shy, you are probably the smartest person in the room, therefore, making you the most interesting person in the room.

What does the word mingle mean to you? Or rather, what does the word mingle make you feel? If you are one of the above-mentioned wallflowers, this might make you a little uncomfortable. However, you don't have to be an introvert to have a very real fear of socializing with people you may not know.

The fear of the unknown has prevented so many people from attending parties and picnics they have been invited to by work colleagues and friends of friends. The question isn't why you don't go, because we all know social anxiety can manifest in many different ways and levels. The question is, why not go?

If the outing involves new and fresh faces, you have an unprecedented opportunity to test all of the skills you have gained in your quest to become charismatic, clever, and likable. What's the worst that can happen? You get a crash course in banter and a chance to show off the newest version of yourself. You see, your current friend group already knows who you were before. Of course, they all probably love the new you, but they may not give you the validation you need and deserve because they are partial to your feelings. Change is never easy, just like making new friends isn't always a walk in the park. Contrary to popular belief, one thing you can never have too many of, is friends.

One particular personality I don't readily trust is a person who says "I like to keep my circle small, so there is less drama." Here's the thing, Barb; you aren't saying *you* prefer to keep your circle small. That's just what happens when you are indeed the drama. I have spent a lifetime avoiding this type of person for no other reason than to avoid having to chase around the drama llama of my friend group.

Small circles limit personal, and sometimes, even professional growth. If you are surrounded by the same people, talking about the same things, how do you expect to grow in all aspects of your life? New friends bring new opportunities; they allow for new adventures and points of view. Imagine being a doctor and only surrounding yourself with medical professionals. The chance of learning anything about the literary world or the business world is slim. While you and your doctor friends may share the same interests, you may not share the same conversational abilities when approached by someone who might not know anything about lung transplants or x-rays. Adding different types of friends to this dynamic is necessary for understanding how others think.

Getting out there is harder than actually being out there. Here are some tips and tricks to convince your inner reticence to buck up and take the road less traveled.

1. Get online: The first way to soothe your shy side is to become part of an online discussion group. These groups vary in topics, promote new and exciting subject matters, and love to have a healthy debate. Some of my favorite people in the world I found online in rooms such as these.

2. Role play is important: Role playing doesn't have to be reserved for some weird bedroom activity. It is actually quite fun to do with prospective friends and even old friends. Learning how you react to breaks in dialogue and the ability to effectively banter back and forth is like literal icing on the cake. This can also increase humility and comedic timing.

3. Reverse the stigma of going out alone: While it can be less distressing to go out with a few friends, and convenient when attending concerts or parties to know someone in the room, this isn't a requirement of going out. Our culture has created an unavoidable reaction to being alone. It tells you that it's not normal when it is absolutely normal. I go to dinner alone and, gasp, even the movies. This doesn't make me pathetic or a loser. It makes me free; free from schedules or friends dragging their feet. I can go where I want to eat, do what I want to do, and enjoy what I like without any distractions. And maybe, just maybe, I will meet a new friend along the way.

The most annoying mental barrier to hanging out by yourself is the completely absurd idea that alone means lonely. Have you ever been at the bar awaiting friends who are running late and found yourself feeling comforted by the fact that they are on their way? This is because you feel like there is a legitimate reason for being there alone. But what if you went out to a bar alone? Would you find yourself feeling like everyone is going to notice that no one is joining you? If so, please do not think it is an abnormal response because, like all learned behavior, bars and restaurants are known for social gatherings of friends.

Let's look at the situation from a different angle. Imagine you are alone at the bar and someone comes up to you and asks, are you waiting for someone? And you reply in the least weird way that you are enjoying a night out alone. To which they reply, why don't you join us? Just like that, you have found yourself in a group of people who want to get to know you. Boom. New friends. You're welcome!

Chapter 6: Charming

"Charm is more valuable than beauty. You can resist beauty, but you cannot resist charm."

— Audrey Tautou

It has been said, to be truly captivating, you must master the skill of interviewing. It sounds odd, I know, but it is a clever way to impart complete interest in someone else, making them feel special and understood. Hear me out.

Have you ever been involved in a conversation with someone new and leave the conversation feeling great about yourself and not sure why? The reason why is simple. The person you just spoke with has mastered something called Social Jiu-Jitsu. They have learned how to get to know you in such a way that they fail to really reveal anything about themselves. Let's look at an example to further your understanding of this clever conversational method.

"Hey there! How are you? Crazy weather we've had lately?"

"Absolutely! It's been insane. What is your favorite season?"

"Oh, Spring for sure. The flowers are blooming, and everyone seems to be happier."

"I absolutely agree. Do you have a favorite flower?"

"Daisies are my favorite. They just make everything beautiful and make great flowers for bouquets. I'm a florist, so I love all flowers, but that one seems to stir my soul."

"Wow, I can really tell you love your job! So, you work locally then?"

"Yes, I have a market right up the road here. We open shortly for the summer season, and I am really excited. You should come to check it out on the 10th. That's opening day!"

"That is so cool you own your own shop! When did you first open? Did it start off successful? With your kind of passion, I have no doubt you killed it!"

"It was slow at first, but by the month's end, we had captivated the neighborhood and have never looked back! Our customers love us for our extreme variety of flowers and homemade goat milk soaps that I make myself with flowers! Right in my own kitchen!"

"Wow, a jack of all trades. You are so interesting! I will come by on the 10th and perhaps stop and smell the roses for a bit!"

You laugh, he laughs, and so begins the start of a new friendship or possibly more? While you spent the whole time talking, what you didn't notice was it was you that was carrying the conversation, not the other way around. You might have even left the conversation a little high off the attention and giddy from the discussion, not realizing you learned nothing about the other person, except that spring is also his favorite season. If so, you've just been body-slammed by an SJJ master, and you couldn't be happier. That is an example of compelling charm. That's an experience that promotes self-esteem and general happiness. But this only works if, while talking to the other person, you are actively listening and responding in such a way that the person you are speaking with doesn't feel rushed or compelled to speak.

The process of Social Jiu-Jitsu is exceedingly difficult, but it can most certainly be learned. While some people have a natural way about them, leaving them always in charge of conversations, others may struggle to move the conversation past small talk. Don't get discouraged. You can always become a magnetic presence with some practice and a whole lot of conversation starters, interview questions, a sincere approach to listening, and understanding when to reveal information without taking over the conversation. Remember, people generally love talking about themselves, especially when they feel comfortable with their listeners.

Chapter 7: Inspiration Revelation

"Don't adapt to the energy in the room. Influence the energy in the room."

— Unknown

Inspiration is what is lacking in today's social culture. With new developments in technologies, people have become controlled by negative influences. For example, Karen's Facebook post about how no matter how many times she complains to McDonald's about her nuggets being cold, they are still cold, and she is calling corporate and getting someone fired. Correct me if I'm wrong, but this sounds like something reserved for coffee conversation between people who like you enough to look beyond the fact that you are brash and overshare far too much.

Karen, like everyone else on Facebook or Instagram, doesn't forget about Twitter. All believe wholeheartedly that people want to know what is going through their minds every minute of every day. I know the ratio of people who feed off her drama is significantly larger than the people that are annoyed by it. But there is another group of people who aren't accounted for, and those people would read one negative post of Karen's drama and delete her. They do this because, unlike the group of people mentioned previously, these people don't need that kind of negativity in their lives.

Optimistic people do not allow pessimistic behavior in their bubble because hope will always be defeated by despair. Dreamers don't like doubt, and positivity will not shine in the face of discouragement. Aspiration will not be forsaken; well, not for the true lights of this world. If you want to be a bright light in the face of a dark world, you have to have priceless positivity.

Positivity is most definitely a personality trait; it is learned from the people around you as you grow, just like that little voice inside your head that knows right from wrong. Positivity is taught to you through parental discipline and actions. If you grow up with an angry father or a rude mother, the chance of you taking on that trait is 80 to 1. That's a huge chance. If you grew up with both parents possessing negative auras, you could count yourself out of being a super likable person; until now.

Whether you had the worst parents in the world or the sweetest parents a child could ask for, that doesn't have to affect the chances of you becoming charismatic, likable, or even clever. While it does mean you will need to remove more dark clutter from your arsenal, it doesn't mean you can't. I mean, some of the most charming and magnetic people had the worst childhoods. The saying "What doesn't kill you makes you funny" is true on a lot of levels. It's an extremely positive outlook on trauma.

That's what positive people do. They take something that hurts and spin it into something that doesn't. Have you ever had a terrible day, and you come across a positive influencer, and they turned something like breaking up into a reason to go to karaoke? That little beam of sunshine talked you into dinner and hours of shouting into a microphone about how you are better off without said lover. Positive people are a gift to society. You would think they carried sunshine in their pockets. And sometimes they do. It's just who they are.

But how do they do it? You might wonder if there is a formula they whip up every day while getting ready to leave the house. I don't know about that but what I do know is there are literally thousands of TED talks, traveling positivity influencers, and blogs about learning to see the bright side of everything.

You might not want to attend a seminar just yet, and I get it. I have some ideas that you can try right now from the comfort of your easy chair and some you can try tomorrow at work or school.

1. Respond, don't react: This goes for over-reacting as well. Try this scenario: How would you react to being fired without warning? Would you become angry or sad, or would you breathe and allow an explanation? Getting fired sucks, but normally when this happens, it's because of loss of passion or lack of promotional advances. Instead of flying off the handle and finding yourself buried in self-loathing, pick yourself up by your bootstraps and find a better job. Now I'm not implying that it won't discourage or dampen your emotions. You should feel the emotions and let them go; they can't harm you if you have released them in a healthy way.

Positive people have the ability to dismiss negativity instead of wallowing in it. That's what makes them such genuinely happy people; they refuse to acknowledge emotional charges after they have put them away.

2. Choose hope over despair: When I was a child, one of my favorite movies was *Pollyanna.* In the movie, Pollyanna is a beam of positivity in the face of adversity. Both of her parents die, and she is forced to move in with her coarse aunt, in a new town and surrounded by people she had never met. One day while shucking beans with the kitchen staff, she tells one of them "I like to find something to be glad about every day." Then she goes on to describe what she was glad about that day. I still think about what she said almost every day, and it has been 30 years since I've watched that movie. The reason I still remember Pollyanna is because of her timeless positivity. She showed me as a child what it is like to be human sunshine. And since that day, I have tried with all my might to live up to Pollyanna standards. Most days I fail, but other days, I bring her sweet spirit with me as a reminder that no matter what is happening to me, there is always room for hope.

3. Practice positive self-talk: We like to say "You are your own worst enemy" and boy, is that the truth. Have you ever felt not good enough or dumb, but no one has said anything of that nature toward you? Well, buckle your seat belts. You are about to ride the Insecurity Train! Insecurity is a faithful friend, isn't it? It knows just when to show up; a date, an event, or a job offer. Let's be honest, sometimes it dictates the clothes you wear and the things you say, tempting you to stay in and watch a movie because what would you bring to the table anyway, right? The way to eliminate the pesky little troll is you must learn to address it. I've found that by naming my insecurity, I am able to address it when in dressing rooms or meeting new

people. It will say, "Wow, that shirt is really tight; I hope when you sit down, you can see your belly rolls." To that, I say. "Shut the heck up, Mildred, you don't even have a body. What do you know about it? Go lay down somewhere, you cow." Then I continue with whatever I was doing. You see, I acknowledged the thought, and aggressively pushed the negative thought out of the picture by telling it to back off. If the thought returns, I will do it again until it becomes a funny dialogue. And just like that, I beat the system. Positive self-talk is the backbone of being a positive person, and everyone needs a positive person in their life. If you can't find one, be one.

Chapter 8: Self-Esteem vs. Arrogance

"Always be a first-rate version of yourself, instead of a second-rate version of somebody else."

-Judy Garland

Self-esteem is something long since described as what you believe about yourself. It is most commonly confused with an ego or being arrogant. But they couldn't be more different; let me explain why.

Self-esteem is defined as confidence in one's own worth or abilities and exhibiting self-respect. Arrogant or egotistical is defined as an exaggerated and unrealistic self-opinion or pride. Self-esteem has really gotten lost over the years, hasn't it? Sometimes, you must go and find it under mountains of aloofness and floating around inside of inflated ego balloons.

Back in my day, self-esteem was actually taught in school; it was meant to be something grand that was specific to you. Like personal goals, you were meant to maintain them and nourish them. Protecting your self-esteem is a talent these days, unlike before when it was a necessity to protect what you believed was your best qualities. And it worked; I can't remember a time in my childhood where my self-esteem was affected by someone else's.

We are now living in an age of sometimes unavoidable comparisons. In the early 90's we didn't know what kind of lives everyone else was living when we weren't around. We didn't know of any updates in salaries or family vacations that seemed too good to be true. I guess that's why our self-esteem stayed relatively high. We didn't have anything to compare it to.

Jealousy has long since been a snake in the grass when it comes to how we perceive ourselves. On the one hand, I might be clever and sometimes interesting. On the other hand, I might be a bit heavier than everyone else at the party. That's called balancing your perceptions. While I might not look like everyone, I have abilities that not everyone has. Balancing your perceptions came a lot easier before the flood of social media and advertising strategies focused on highlighting more of what you don't have than what you do have.

Have you ever found yourself on a social media site thinking "Wow, they seem to have it all, money, looks, the perfect kids"? Then all of a sudden, you feel a pang of insecurity followed by a feeling of embarrassment surrounding your own life and what you have or don't have? If so, it doesn't make you a self-loathing martyr; it's just envy waking up and stretching her legs.

Jealousy and Envy aren't the same people. Envy is maybe a second cousin to Jealousy because one is malicious and has destructive properties, while the other is more acquisitive and desiring. To say I am envious of best-selling authors doesn't necessarily mean I don't like successful authors or myself. Jealous people tend to be very insulting toward people they want to be like; they like to seem above it all. Crude jealousy can be dated back to the first human beings and the direct cause of many cultures to be wiped out solely because one side wanted something the other side possessed.

This leads us back to arrogance. This behavior is like self-esteem's abusive stepdad, who can't find his beer or car keys. Arrogance is just another way of inflated self-importance. While self-esteem focuses on positive affirmations, arrogance focuses on self-absorption. Some of the people affected by arrogance often take the phrase "Fake it till you make it" to extremes. They often create an alternate universe in their mind that allows for the confidence in talent but not the actual skills to obtain said talent.

Arrogant characters can be found loitering around poker tables, spewing advice and information, but when a chair becomes available to play, they all of a sudden have somewhere to be. Why? Because they have such a high opinion of themselves that if they sat down and lost or weren't good at all, it would expose their vulnerability and who they actually are.

The quickest way to become someone no one wants to be around is to try and manipulate the people around you. Human beings are born with instinct, and that superpower can spot a phony a mile away. My advice to anyone suffering from "Blowhard Syndrome" is to rewire the thought of being better than someone. Superiority is not a disorder. It's a practice and just like everything else, you have to practice a behavior free of condescension, adding more compassion and benevolence to your bag of tricks, because being a jack of all trades is a lie. If you've ever read the full quote connected to that phrase, it goes like this. "A jack of all trades is a master of none." And that's a fact, Jack.

Chapter 9: Captivate Your Audience

"Mirror, mirror on the wall. Who's the fairest of them all?"

—Walt Disney

It doesn't necessarily take an actor or author to captivate people. Writers and performers have just learned techniques to draw people's attention with whatever it is they have to offer. Whether it be an actor's great stage presence or an author's incredible ability to create vivid imagery. They have developed those things over time; no author is a best-selling author right out of the gate, and no actor has become famous in their acting studio. Everything takes practice, even when it's becoming the main character in your own life.

Have you ever asked yourself "Am I the most important thing in my life?" It's a weird question but one that should be, and eventually will be, asked of yourself. We spend so much time wanting to be the main character in others' lives that we forget we have to be number one in our own existence. And if you haven't asked yourself recently who your protagonist is, I will ask you to do that now.

If your husband or wife comes to mind, or your children or work, you are not putting yourself first. How do you plan on captivating an entire group of people when you can't even captivate yourself? You most certainly can't and won't; here's why.

Let me be completely transparent with you here because false confidence is glaringly obvious. I've said it before and will say it again. You cannot trick people into liking or respecting you. At one point or another, the other shoe will drop, and you will be exposed as a closet narcissist. The quickest way to get labeled a sociopath is to get caught not being who you say you are. You must connect with people on a cosmic level, not a pseudo level, and it's not hard to do if you are authentically you. That only comes by liking yourself, respecting yourself, and treating yourself well. To do that, you must accept who you are and who you want to be, which you are already doing by reading this book. Pat yourself on the back for taking the steps toward becoming a beacon of sunshine.

I urge you to get to know yourself a little better, so everyone else can. Then develop the tools to introduce yourself to others as a comfortable and charming friend. Here are some ways to captivate an audience without even trying.

1. Take the initiative: Make a toast, start a group conversation, or throw a themed party. In doing so, you can bring your personality to life without sounding boastful or overbearing.

2. Don't force it: Speaking of overbearing, avoid speaking over people, making inappropriate jokes, and needing to be front and center. Hang back, read the room, and jump in when you feel you have enough attention to successfully execute a funny anecdote or story.

3. Be interesting: Life is nothing but a collection of stories. Experiences are what make legends, so experience things. And if you don't have a lot of eventful things in your bag of tricks, make them up. No one will know the difference.

And have fun, like real fun. Never stay on the sidelines watching others have fun—get out there and experience life. Until you do, you will have to live by a script instead of a story.

Chapter 10: Conversation Intelligence

"The true sign of intelligence is not knowledge but imagination."

—Albert Einstein

Have you ever found yourself at a party on the edge of a discussion you knew absolutely nothing about, hoping and praying no one asked what your opinion is on the subject? I have, and it's not fun at all. Sometimes I wonder "What do these people do, research a specific topic in hopes of presenting it at a party or over dinner?" Do they know they are being show-offs, seeing that no one is really following what they are discussing? Most of the patrons are asking more questions rather than joining in on the conversation. These people are called "Blowhards," and blowhards don't care if you understand the topic; they only care if you are interactive. Meaning they want you to be confused, so they appear to be smarter than you; they also thrive off being the educator. Believe it or not, when people feel better than others, they feel better about themselves.

Narcissistic behavior is no way to retain popularity amongst your peers. Remember before when I said, "Sometimes people don't realize they are annoying"? That holds true for blowhards; they are naturally overconfident and off-putting.

These types of personalities are hard to swallow due to their uncontrollable word vomit and inability to admit when they are wrong. So, they become aggravated in debates and intellectual banter.

Steer clear of overdoing it by relying more on your actual intelligence than the footnotes you've written on your palm or cheat sheet. Substantial intelligence has longevity; it should be subtle and low-key. When explaining something to read or hear, be careful not to lead the conversation; allow for others to weigh in or ask questions. In doing this, you become less of a teacher and more of a teammate, which is a more vulnerable approach. Vulnerable as a definition is often misrepresented. It is usually defined as weak or sensitive. Therapists have been trying to fix this for years. The true definition of vulnerable is accessible, liable, and wide open. Not one of those words depicts a weak human being. The movie industry is to blame, as they portray a lot of common misconceptions.

Creating an illusion doesn't quite make it true, now does it? When you approach a conversation with an open mind and consideration, you construct a positive environment, one that is all-inclusive and creative. You will find that the reaction and perception are remarkably different than going into it with an overbearing attitude.

I had someone say to me once "I am more attracted to intelligent people. They always fascinate me, and there is nothing better than a night full of stories shared between two people of like minds and a bottle of wine." Now I don't know if she ever found her Resourceful Romeo or not, but I hope wherever she is, she is talking about the Milky Way with someone who understands the importance of the stars just as she does. I am certain she had to go through her share of blowhards, as we all do, but I hope she came out triumphant in the end.

Conversation intelligence doesn't have to be so black and white; it has many levels. On one hand, you could be smart in the subject of dinosaurs. On the other, you may be able to recite a poem or sitcom reference. People are so different and versatile. One day you might find someone who doesn't know what Seinfeld is, and you could be their knight in shining Kramer, introducing her to one of the funniest shows to ever grace the television screen. This will sequentially make you clever and funny and a great judge of character, quite literally.

The take here is to become conversationally intelligent. You have to have something that makes you extraordinary and authentically rare. Everyone has an ability that sets them apart from everyone else. If we didn't, we would be an entire population that understands physics. Do you understand physics? Yeah, me either, but what I do know is how to construct a poem or book and even tell a vivid story. These are things that make up my charm and aesthetic; they make me interesting enough to appeal to the masses and genuinely likable. While these things are not the only reason people like me, they are great conversation starters "Hey, what do you do for a living?" "I write books for a living." "Oh really, what kinds of books? I love books! Do you write fiction or nonfiction? What's your favorite book?" And so on.

I have met some of the most interesting people, many that are way more interesting than myself. The thing that sets these people apart from the herd is confidence. Confidence is key to charm; it is key to brilliance and inspiration. You wouldn't receive surgery from a doctor who was kind of knowledgeable about bladders? No, you want a doctor who was confident in his abilities to fix your bladder because of the intelligence gained throughout years of performing surgery. The same holds true with conversational intelligence.

Part Two

During a college seminar about person perception, I was asked "What do I believe others think of me or remember me for?" I quickly announced, "I hope it's my sense of humor; if it's not that, I would say it's that I wear pajamas in public." My professor didn't skip a beat "Are you wearing pajamas right now?" I replied "No sir, this is just a faded jumpsuit with a Christmas Donald Duck hanging ornaments. It's the latest fashion." The class literally detonated with laughter, and my professor took a couple of minutes to recover, then stated "Well, I can say with complete faith it may be both. Congratulations on understanding your essential self at such a young age." I tipped an imaginary hat, and we carried on with class. I made three new friends that day and earned respect from a professor who was known for his callousness toward students.

The moral of the story is the most interesting people are those who know and understand their true selves. They know how to read the room and transition from one attribute to the other depending on what's needed at the very time it's needed. Alas, this isn't something that comes easy for everyone.

Chapter 11: The Self Awareness Test

"The only questions that really matter are the ones you ask yourself."

— Ursula K. Le Guin

If you're not completely sure who you are, you are not alone. In a recent study among college students, 48% of the students who participated had absolutely no clue what they wanted to do with their lives. Keep in mind the study was done across the board, from incoming freshmen to senior graduates. Considering that statistic is nearly half, you might ask "But how can that be? Isn't college where you find your passion and develop the tools needed to succeed as functional adults?" Wrong. "But you go to college based on what you want to do for the rest of your life." Wrong. Do you know how many college-graduates sleep in the basement of their parents' houses long after graduation? I don't know the true statistic, but I am sure it's up there with college dropouts which is nearly 60% of students who attend directly after high school.

The reason behind these wild numbers is simple; you are not taught in school how to differentiate between the needs of your parents and your actual needs. While you may be intelligent enough to become a doctor, it doesn't necessarily mean you aspire to be one. Time after time, year after year, students unavoidably follow in the footsteps of their parents because they do not have a definitive idea of who they are, unattached from their parents.

Fun Fact: Your parents are solely responsible for that little voice inside your head. You know, the one that tells you the difference between right and wrong? Or the one that guides you through tough life choices? Most of your core values and decision-making skills have been transplanted there by your parents. The saying "A mother never truly leaves her children, not even in death, because her words live on in the hearts of her children" is most likely referring to this theory.

More often than not, parents want the best for their children but not realizing they are micromanaging them. Being a parent myself, I catch myself saying "Have you thought about what you want to do after high school?" While it may seem harmless, what I am actually doing is placing pressure on my children to decide their future with an unreasonable timeline. Children's brains aren't even fully developed at graduation, not even close. The human brain isn't fully developed until the age of 25, so why do we put so much pressure on 17- and 18-year-olds to determine the rest of their lives, knowing they don't even have the intellectual tools to effectively do so?

This holds true for self-definition as well. How does a person define themselves without the adequate tools to do so? If you're one of the lucky ones who have higher self-realization sooner in life than others, you have subconsciously already predetermined who you are. But don't get cocky just yet; just as the flowers bloom in the spring, they die in the winter. Personalities can change just like the seasons and sometimes that quick. Who you are in June can be different than who you are in December. We are movable trees; we are always growing and transforming. Here are some exercises you can do to find out who you are right now.

Find a place where you will be undisturbed for about an hour: If you do not answer these questions with full unadulterated honesty, you are cheating no one but yourself.

1. If there were no consequences to your actions, how would you act?

2. What are three of your most important core values?

3. If you had to describe yourself in three words, what would they be?

4. If others were to describe you in three words, what do you think those three words would be?

5. Are you self-confident or self-deprecating?

6. Do you like who you are?

7. Do you wish to be a certain way? More humorous, classy, or assertive?

8. Are you satisfied with your career? If not, why?

9. Whose dream was it to do what you are doing?

10. Do you feel as if you can change?

These basic questions can effectively gauge where you are in the eyes of, well, you. Be careful to not confuse that with what others think of you. A common mistake in character development is the thought of what people expect of me or developing a people-pleasing mentality. You are the only person that controls your own happiness. Believe it or not, people can't read your mind; they only react to how you treat them. For instance, if you are rude, people will call you rude. It's as simple as that.

Chapter 12: Embrace Your Weirdness

"Where's your will to be weird?"

— Jim Morrison

When I was in third grade, my teacher called my mother in for an impromptu parent-teacher conference. Fear spread across my chest like a California wildfire when I heard the news. For the life of me, I couldn't figure out what I had done wrong that warranted getting my mother involved. Patiently I waited for my fate outside the sound-proof classroom door until my mother came to take me home.

The absence of immediate condemnation had me in a state of perpetual fright and confusion. When I tell you, I jumped out of my skin every time that woman made the slightest movement, believe it. Her stone-cold silence was deafening, to say the least, but what worried me more is why she was so quiet. The silent treatment is my mother's version of waterboarding; she would wait for you to break the silence then proceed to rain hell's fire upon our heads. But on this particular day, she didn't seem angry or disappointed, so out of sheer confusion and mental exhaustion, I began to cry.

My mother noticed my sobs from the backseat and pulled the car over. She asked me if I ever heard of the term Attention Disorder. I shook my head then assured her I do listen in class. I wasn't lying; I spent the better part of my days trying to focus on my teacher's voice rather than the constant pencil tapping and feet shuffling behind me. My mother wasn't giving me the silent treatment at all; she just didn't know what to say. Without another word, she opened her door, then mine, and proceeded to hug me around my neck so hard I thought it might snap in two.

At the time, I didn't understand what she meant by "kids like me" or why she was so upset. What I didn't hear through the thick classroom doors was my teacher going over my attention deficit diagnosis and attempting to explain this to my mother in a way that didn't make her feel excluded or confused. If I could go back to that point in time, I might ask my teacher why she couldn't have had the same respect for me? After that day, I was removed from my classmates and placed in a small bland room with one other student who was known for eating his own boogers, and there I stayed until middle school beside Slow Steven, trying not to watch him pick at his butt every time he got up to sharpen his pencil.

I can joke about it now, but that day was one of my mother's hardest days as a parent. She just wanted me to feel normal, accepted, and unafraid of the wicked world. But nothing could have prepared her for the life I would eventually live. A life full of acceptance and service to people just like me; people who need me and my experiences to help them along the way, just like she did for me.

Thanks, mom.

Chapter 13: The Art of Listening

"When people talk, listen completely. Most people never listen."

— Ernest Hemingway

One of the sincerest forms of respect is actually listening to what another has to say. This is key in building a strong foundation to becoming a more likable person. The practice of Active Listening is scientifically proven to mold how people react to you.

Ralph G. Nichols once said, "The most basic human need is the need to understand and to be understood. The best way to understand people is to listen to them." I'm going to go ahead and say it. This is indisputably the most brilliant take on social interactions I have ever come across. The simplicity of it all is mind-blowing. Nichols is justifiably known as the "Father of Listening." In 1948, he developed what is now known as the most prolific process for active listening.

What is active listening? Active listening is the process of listening attentively while someone else is talking, paraphrasing, and reflecting on what they have said, withholding judgment and advice. Sounds easy, right? In my own experience, this was absolutely torturous to learn, and I am still learning. Being alert and engaged with the conversation is how you combat the inconsistency of your attention span.

Have you ever been speaking to someone, whether it be over the phone or in-person, and while they are speaking, you are actively analyzing what they are saying or, worse, not listening at all? After they are done speaking, they will undoubtedly ask you what you think about what they just explained. At this point, you scramble to find keywords or a clear definition to which they were just speaking. Unless you are Spock, you will not be able to retrace the past quick enough to come up with a reasonable answer, and in turn, your credibility will take a hit.

Active listening is harder than it sounds, at least in my journey. I was diagnosed with ADHD at age ten. If you're not familiar with the symptoms of attention deficit hyperactivity disorder, I will quickly educate you. ADHD is on the other side of the spectrum when it comes to listening and understanding, and that's putting it lightly. So, you can imagine how hard it was to get my neurodivergent brain to comply with Ralph Nichols course instructions. As a matter of fact, I had to attempt it once a month for 24 months just to get the first four steps down. Give me a break. My brain type has the word divergent in it. The definition of divergent is literally: diverging, differing, deviating. Deviating! Come on, man, I'm lucky to even be involved in conversations. Do you know that one person standing in front of you at the grocery store? Who, when the line is moving, they remain standing where they are, and you awkwardly have to tap them and say the line is moving. I am, said human being. Daydreaming is hard-wired into my DNA; to change that, I have to be on top of my game at all moments.

If you long to become someone people love talking to, there are steps you can take to reduce the chance of looking like a blowhole at the end of a lecture or conversation or even a first date. If you're like me and speaking engagements have left you traumatized in one way or the other, for the love of Pete, try and pay attention to the next few steps.

1. Face the person who is speaking to you: Eye contact is the first indication that you are listening and participating.

2. Be attentive and responsive: This can be as easy as shaking your head or nodding or even quick responses such as "Yes" or "I understand."

3. Keep an open mind: Try and keep any judgments or opinions to the back of your mind. Thoughts like these can interrupt concentration, and you could miss key parts of the discussion.

4. Listen to key phrases and settings: Try and picture what they are talking about without daydreaming or interrupting.

5. Ask questions: Only to further your understanding.

To effectively increase your value as a listener or shoulder to cry on, you have to have the true ability to convey empathy. Being sensitive to the other person's hardships, joyfulness, or pain is the main component to becoming an invaluable source of refuge to the people around you. If you are not sympathetic in nature, this can be incredibly hard to pull off. It takes a lot of energy and concentration. Active listening is a generous way to show people you understand their feelings and facilitates great communication moving forward in your interpersonal relationships.

Chapter 14: Confidence Champion! Ding-Ding!

"Insecurity is the enemy of wit."

— Unknown

Confidence is thought to be responsible for 20% of knowledge. Knowledge is something that becomes hard-wired; it's not something that you can lose, like a job or a status. Once you have learned something, most of the time, you retain it forever. Take riding a bike, for instance; once you've learned how to ride a bike throughout your life, you can easily pick up a bike and ride it; the same goes for swimming. Intelligence is a lot like riding a bike when you think of it literally. Logistically it's a bit more complex. But no matter how you present it, it all works the same. When I was starting my English career, there were a few things that I just could not retain. Like what's a forceful verb and how to get it banned from the English language because it is the most unnecessary reason to give someone a C- on an exam and ruin the chance of acing the class. I let that one get away from me. Let's resume.

Taking into consideration that experience grows knowledge, it also grows confidence. You can spend six years in a classroom learning, but learning is not knowledge no matter what they tell you in high school. Synonyms of knowledge are as follows: Ability, philosophy, proficiency, and familiarity. Oh, and don't forget wisdom. Wisdom is earned. It is developed over time and is indispensable. It is vital to know the difference. Learning is simply a process of training the mind. When you understand what you have learned and have put it to use in the form of experiences, you can grow knowledge which solidifies confidence.

Although anyone can attain it, confidence is the easiest trait to mimic. Mimicking behavior is a part of all human DNA. It starts when we are babies and continues until death. When we are babies, this allows us to make sounds and faces and, of course, learn how to speak. When we grow, we learn the ability to copy others' quips and phrases, growing our personality.

When something or someone is funny, we laugh, then try the same bit to make others laugh. I used to know a guy that emulated Jim Carrey so much that he did the most convincing Jim Carrey stand-up ever and still does it to this day.

When it comes to being a master conversationalist, you must incorporate confidence, intelligence, and crisp well-worded stories to draw attention to yourself. Think about the most amusing stories from your life and use them as your go-to stories in conversations.

The road to complete confidence is marred with self-doubt and fear of rejection. Most of us feel insecure sometimes. What you're not supposed to do is feel insecure all the time. The following three types of insecurities are the most common forms and can help you along your path to overcoming the negative beliefs that you have about yourself.

Insecurity due to recent rejection or failure: One of the biggest negative augments when it comes to self-esteem is a recent break-up or death of a loved one or job loss. Unhappiness is directly related to self-esteem. A recent study on happiness suggests that up to 40% of our "happiness quota" is determined by recent hits to your pride. That's why you spiral after losing someone or something. Instead, take my earlier advice about positivity and pick yourself up, and remember you are in charge of how people perceive you. Do you want to be a ray of sunshine or a dark cloud? The answer is up to you.

Insecurity due to social anxiety: Some people feel social anxiety at parties, work events, and even interviews. Social anxiety, in a nutshell, is the fear of being evaluated by others—and deemed to be lacking. This causes you to feel anxious and self-conscious. Have you ever had to stand in front of a crowd, whether it be a presentation or interview, and began feeling like your clothes are not acceptable, or your hair looks silly? Then you begin pulling your shirt down or fidgeting with your hair, this insecurity manifesting. Many of my clients describe being bullied or harassed in high school because of this exclusion; it still negatively affects their adult life. Social anxiety generally distorts your self-worth and prevents you from exhibiting your true self. If you suffer from moderate social anxiety, the best advice I can give is, do something. Get out there. This means accept invitations and get out of your comfort zone. Be a wallflower for a while, test the waters. But do not remain on the sidelines. Choose to be bold over boring!

Insecurity due to lack of emotional security: Emotional security is the measure of the stability of an individual's emotional state. Emotional insecurity can leave a person feeling uneasy and vulnerable in relationships or social environments. Jealousy is a product of emotional insecurity. When you feel unworthy or beneath your partner, you automatically begin to worry they will find someone else. Or your boss will hire someone else because you're not good enough at your job. Emotional insecurity can be alleviated by progressive resilience. Resilience is the power of a person's ability to bounce back after disappointment or damage to the ego. If you feel like you suffer from a lack of emotional security, try some of these activities to help you bounce back from bad vibes.

1. Keep a journal: Write down all the reasons you feel undesirable. Evaluate yourself on how much effort you put into changing your personal condition. Set goals and congratulate yourself as you tackle all the negative thoughts.

2. Therapy: Therapy can be a great outlet free of judgments and fear. Tell your therapist why you feel this way and allow him or her to guide you through the storm. Everyone needs a therapist, so don't feel like a failure for not being able to 100% fix yourself. If therapy isn't for you, try meditation or exercise to promote body and mind positivity!

Don't be so critical of yourself or anyone else. Everyone has flaws, some way more than others, but we all have them. Self-confidence is the hardest thing to control in the human brain. Insecurity is a powerful emotion that distorts your way of seeing yourself. But just like my mom used to say "I wish you could see yourself through my eyes, then you would see how absolutely beautiful and talented you really are." So, in honor of my sweet mother, seize the day with a smile and cultivated confidence.

Chapter 15: Admiration is Free

"I can live for two months on a good compliment."

— Mark Twain

I wrote an essay once for a pretty well-known author. She then paid me for my services and closed out the job. She didn't give much feedback and left me high and dry when it came to know what she thought of it. I knew, of course, she had to like it, or I would've not received payment. But I felt uneasy about not receiving feedback. Quick side note: writers, no matter what scale of success, have a constant need for the positive feedback. I'm sure it's a disorder we all share on some level. Mark Twain described it brilliantly when he said, like all writers "I can live for two months on a good compliment." After a few months passed, I was offered a full-time position as an assistant writer for this best-selling author, and that was all the feedback I needed; and let me tell you, I rode that welcome wagon until the wheels fell off.

The moral of that story is compliments don't always have to be said to be understood. There are plenty of ways to give compliments. Mine came in the form of a job; others may come in the form of touch, interest, and the most used, positive feedback or admiration. Let's go through some of the ways people compliment each other.

1. Tokens of Appreciation: This doesn't have to be super expensive, like a diamond necklace or anything. Who do you think you are, Warren Buffett? Don't get so ahead of yourself; gestures are little hints of affection or mutual respect (if it's a relationship). Think more along the lines of an impromptu picnic; or if she likes gardening, buys her some seed packets instead of store-bought flowers and offer to assist her in planting them. If it's a friendship or coworker, think of a gift card or a lunch date to catch up or just hang out.

2. Let her/him pick: A good way to compliment someone's taste is to ask them to pick a movie, restaurant, or vacation destination. Something like "You always pick the best movies." Or "You have great taste in clothes, what do you think I should buy?" This creates a confidence boost and shows you respect and admire them.

3. Touch: There is a fine line between comfort and creepy; let's keep this tactic more Santa Claus and less Ted Bundy. When using touch as a language, you should never shy away from a hug or shaking hands. These are key in building comfortable relationships. But like all things, read the room and person before touch; some people don't like touch, and you will see that from body language. Over time you will see that even someone that doesn't like warm hugs will allow you to throw your arm over their shoulder or high five you!

4. Show Respect: When someone demonstrates mutual respect for another, they are showing they not only care for others, but they also care for themselves. Respect is the most prominent expression of praise. It is in itself a way of showing the other person just how invaluable you are to them. If you

don't respect someone, how can you like them? It is impossible—the two must come hand in hand.

5. Admiration: This is the most common way and the easiest way to show appreciation. "Your hair looks great today, Lacey!" "Thanks, I just got it done. Not looking so bad yourself, Jack!" or something less physical. "You have a great sense of humor!" And so on. Giving compliments should never be forced. If you don't feel it, don't say it. People can tell the difference between sarcasm and condescension; neither is honest nor appreciated. Keep it light and keep it classy, and you will slowly become someone everyone wants to be around!

Chapter 16: Shoulders Are for Coats, Not Chips

"I hid that chip on your shoulder so that you'll never find it. Because without it, you're so much more interesting."

— Unknown

We have covered what it's like to be a positive influence, and how to build self-confidence, and also what role self-esteem plays in all of this. But the beginning of all of these things is Self-Talk. Self-talk is the culmination of rational and irrational thought. I know you have heard of "Yin and Yang." Western civilization kind of indulges in the sense of determining the difference between right and wrong. And the phrase "Black and White" also suggests that a grey area shouldn't exist in the realm of good and evil.

Take what we know about angels who sit upon shoulders and somehow deter bad choices into consideration. What are they actually doing? And are they metaphorical or not?

When I was a child, I often wondered if I was missing one of my angels, only to realize I didn't actually have two. You see, yin and yang aren't separate forces. If you look at a picture of a yin and yang, you will see they are part of the same entity.

So, the dueling angel theory isn't quite accurate, is it? But this isn't an essay about if you believe in tiny angels or not. It's about conscious thought. Conscious thought is a thought you are aware of. Unlike subconscious thought, which is done without your consent. If you take the two different thoughts and compare them to two different angels or black and white, boom, you get figurative symbolism.

An example of self-talk or conscious thought is when you are waiting on the results of an exam to be released. You have a general idea of how well you did, but you don't actually know for sure. There will be two thoughts that stand out more than any. The thought of "Of course you passed. You've worked so hard! Stop worrying so much. You've got this!" Then sometimes immediately, the happy thought is followed by a more sinister voice, with the not-so-good news. "How could you possibly pass? You went out on Saturday and missed a whole night of studying. You are definitely going to fail."

What the human mind doesn't want to do, is agree, and this causes a state of never-ending internal conflict between what you know and what you are being told. Positive self-talk can be just the armor you need against insecurities, which can be defined as the little devil who antagonizes the little angel. Insecurities can make you feel unworthy of a lot of things affecting every aspect of your life.

Your love life: If you feel unworthy of love and attachment due to insecurities, such as what you look like or things you have been through.

Your work life: If you feel undereducated or not as productive as other employees, you may not apply for many promotions.

In your friendships: If you feel like you bring less to the table than some of your more witty or clever friends, you may not jump in on conversations for fear you may be laughed at or ignored.

These little pangs of anxiety can control the way you perceive yourself if you allow them to. One way to combat your inner critic is to practice positive self-talk. When a negative thought pops up, quickly show it to the door. Force it to see you the way you should be seen, in great lighting. This, like any self-help method, will take a bit of practice.

Chapter 17: How to Combat Your Inner Cartoonist: A Guide to Erasing Self-Doubt

"The worst enemy to creativity is self-doubt."

— Sylvia Plath

By naming these intrusive thought bubbles, you can find their true origin. The most shocking revelation you will have during this process is how many of those thoughts aren't actually said by you. The only way to seek and destroy is to define these doubters that live in the dark parts of your brain.

What I mean by that is you must find out where it originated. Don't get me wrong, you could just be self-sabotaging, but history has shown that most of the time, that little voice doesn't actually belong to you, but someone who raised you or hurt you in the past. If you have a chatty Kathy or a trauma Thomas whispering bitter tangents in your ear, the most efficient way to quiet them is to define them.

1. "You're not wearing that skirt out of this house! What will the neighbors say? You're sending the wrong message to the boys." Does this sound familiar? This is mental abuse from a

father or mother, who repeatedly suggested that you were being too sexy or embarrassing. "What will the neighbors say?" These kinds of statements have the capacity to dig into your subconscious due to the not-so-underlining suggestion that everyone is watching and judging you based on your choice of clothing. This is the quickest way to plant the seed of doubting your own fashion sense and causing anxiety every time you walk out of your house.

2. "You aren't applying yourself enough. You can do better. Did you even prepare for the test?" "I've chosen someone else for the promotion; he/she has better qualifications." Or "She thinks she will actually get the job!" *insert obnoxious water cooler laughter*

These comments have been said to everyone who has ever gone to school or participated in any race for a raise in the workplace. Needless to say, it doesn't feel good for your commitment to be doubted in any capacity, let alone when a teacher decides "You can do better" when you obviously cannot. If you studied day and night for seven days for a test and you still got a C+, then that's your capability, and that's okay; your competence doesn't have to be 100%. When it comes to healthy work ethics, some people may be lacking a sense of forbearance. You must remember you work with these people; you are not friends with these people. That's why you refer to these individuals as acquaintances. But that doesn't mean these associates can't hurt you or add to your self-doubt. When someone talks behind your back, it can tarnish your self-confidence and leave you feeling less like a winner and more like a stooge and imminent failure.

3. "You're such a fake person; you think no one can tell, but everyone talks about you when you leave the room. I can't take you anywhere. Do you plan on wearing that tonight? I'm the only person who could ever love you or understand you. Why are you so stupid?"

If any of these comments set off loud alarms in your ears, it means at one point or another, you have been a victim of verbal abuse or bullying. This can come from siblings; yes, they can cause very lasting effects long after the abuse stops. Or a husband/partner or friend. When someone is being downright critical or speaking out of anger, they use words to try and control the other person. This leaves the victim questioning who they are and wondering if the harsh words were indeed true. When someone you love and respect defines you as self-absorbed, inadequate, or worthless, you are left reorganizing what you know and what you are being labeled as.

"Am I fake? Am I annoying? I honestly thought this outfit was nice looking. Should I not wear this color?" These are intense questions of self-worth and can damage years' worth of positive self-talk in mere seconds.

PSA: Don't be the kind of person who breaks down the sensitive parts of people for entertainment or control. The end result is even after you have left the relationship, the person you emotionally traumatized has a bigger "Yin than Yang," throwing off the delicate balance of who they are and what they have been told they are.

The number of people abused in the world has tripled in the last century or so. The reason behind this wild jump in statistics might surprise you. Most people assume that if they were victims of emotional or verbal abuse, they'd know it, right? That couldn't be less true. When describing verbal abuse, you use terms like yelling, belittling, or name-calling. While these descriptions are accurate, there is more to verbal and emotional abuse than what meets the eyes.

For example, you and your significant other are at dinner, and you are in stitches over a joke you made in the breakroom today and explaining how your co-workers reacted. You try and make eye contact promoting involvement from the other side of the table, and are met with uninterested eyes "Where did you hear the joke? Did you come up with it on your own? No, that's not possible. We both know you are not clever enough for that." Not only did your partner shut down any further conversation flow by using the silent treatment method. They also insulted your credibility. So, the next time you find yourself in a situation that calls for humor, you avoid taking part, for fear you might not be as clever as you once thought. There is nothing worse than feeling like the recipient of pity laughing.

Chapter 18: Don't Clean Up Messes You Didn't Make

"Don't judge yourself by what others did to you."

— C. Kennedy, Ómorphi

Verbal abuse can all but destroy a human being's ability to grow and build a solid foundation on which their personalities can flourish. If you feel like you have or are being emotionally assaulted in any way, please seek help. Ask for the opinions of those around you because, in most cases of internal abuse, the evidence can't be seen by the naked eye. But changes in behavior and communication will be noticeable by family and friends. The most common sign of emotional abuse is becoming withdrawn and cynical. Someone who used to be extremely adept now stays quiet, unsure of what to say or what people will think of what they say. That's a chip of anxiety unnecessarily placed upon the shoulder of who you used to be. Now that you know how to define that heavy voice who is hell-bent on ruining your day, here are a couple of ideas to combat negative self-talk with positive, inspiring talk:

When in doubt, go out: Never let what you are wearing or how you feel about what you're wearing keep you from attending that concert or party. The reality isn't that no one will have an opinion. That's unrealistic. But the chances of any rude comments said under breaths will surely be outweighed by the positive ones said to your face. Unless someone is directly trying to control your mood, they usually don't insult people for the sake of doing so. So, get out there and rock that frilly skirt; it's vintage, and everyone loves vintage!

Never pass on a laugh: Let me tell you something I am absolutely certain of. Funny people are the first people to get invited to any occasion. I used to think I was considered the token "Funny One." This is a form of self-talk. I figured if I wasn't the "Mom" of the group or the infamous "D-D" of the group, I held a sort of a leading role in my group of friends. And being the funny one isn't the worst title I could have. Have you met the "Hot Mess"? This one can be found leaning against the bar, awkwardly winking at strangers, or riding the mechanical bull so many times we are forced to explain why there is puke on everyone standing near it. Or "The Fighter," the one who has two drinks, then suddenly assumes everyone at the bar is giving side-eye. The fighter is a loose cannon, the hot mess is the worst, but the funny one is dependable; imagine being compatible with all personalities. I mean, who's going to tell the hot mess story the next day with the precision of a stand-up comedian? That's right, the funny one.

Give yourself a break: A lot of people can't sing; that doesn't keep them from singing. A lot of people can't run a marathon, but that doesn't keep them from entering the race. And a lot of people have been told they aren't good enough, but that doesn't prevent them from trying. Not everyone is going to like you. That's a fact of life. A lesser-known fact is you don't always have to care. Practice talking to yourself with the same energy you use to build everyone around you up. Compliments are the fruit of the human experience. Try sharing some of the grapes with yourself.

Chapter 19: You Shouldn't Have a Comfort Zone; You Are Not Furniture

"If we were meant to stay in one place, we'd have roots instead of feet…"

— Rachel Wolchin

Your comfort zone is officially closed for repairs; proceed to the nearest detour. Your detour is a direct path between where you are and where you want to be. Just like driving down a long boring interstate on the way to your fabulous beach vacation, you have to get through the plains of Oklahoma before you see any palm trees or seagulls. And sometimes you get lost and have to ask for directions. When you do find this book and read it again, keep going until you reach the sandy beaches of self-understanding and acceptance.

Throughout this book, I have spoken a lot about self-love and self-exploration. The real reason for the repetition is not to convince you to love yourself but rather to love yourself first. If you do not love the person you are, how on earth do you expect others to love you? When you don't actively love yourself, it doesn't matter what kind of intelligence you bring to the table or how funny you can be at a party. The absence of love creates darkness you may not even notice but trust me, others do.

It isn't a matter of charisma or likeability at this point because some of the biggest and funniest comedians in history have fell victim to pretending to result in tragedy. The dangers of hiding behind big smiles and quippy comebacks are clearer now than they have ever been. That's why I find myself repeating self-love over and over in my teachings to avoid a situation where I give you all the tools to convince others to love you, but not the tools to convince you to love you.

A fact of life is you may not always appreciate what gifts and talents you have. You won't always like what you see in the mirror or other opinions you might have about what makes you likable. But you will always have the ability to change; to change your attitude, your perception, and even your image. I have rebranded myself at least 10 different times in 30 years. Why? Because when I found myself uncomfortable with something I was lacking, whether it be intelligence or personal pride and even the ability to stand out, I changed that feeling.

You are not stuck in the mind you were born into. The mind is complicated and intricate, yes, but it isn't unexplorable. Contrary to popular belief, changing the way you see yourself is a mindful transformation. A transformation that doesn't involve any physical properties because you aren't changing on the outside. You are changing your genetic make-up and washing away years of self-deprecation without the need for a soapy loofa. Here are some tips for changing your genetic make-up to a softer shade of yellow.

Develop a personal mantra: Mantras have a spiritual-like force behind them. They remind you of your goals and personal perspective. Try something like "You can do anything you put your mind to." Or one of my favorites "Keep going."

Count joys and blessings: This is the easiest way to come back down to earth or to rise from the depths of depression or any negative affirmations. Remind yourself of all you have and all that love you.

Savor all things positive: Breathe in accomplishments like air; allow happiness to linger long after the fact. Set goals, and when you accomplish that goal, cherish it and pat yourself on the back and then set another! No one has ever been told they were way too happy, so embrace it as much as you can.

Allow your inner child to guide you: Give the reigns to your sense of wonder every once in and a while and allow that sense of adventure to take you places far away from disappointment. Rely on that innocence and simplicity to change the way you see the world, even if it's for a short while.

Master your moods: Create a mood chart and track your moods daily. This can give a sense of patterns in behaviors and what environmental elements may have contributed to the change in attitude. Instead of being a servant to your ever-changing moods, you can now become the ruler of your kingdom of joyfulness.

Proactive mental health is the way you approach what makes you unique and protecting it. Growing up with ADHD and anxiety in the '80s wasn't easy, so I developed certain coping skills that made me stand out like a sore thumb amongst my peers. Had proactive mental health been a thing back then, I may not have been confused with disorders such as oppositional defiant disorder, bipolar disorder, or my personal favorite, Tourette's syndrome. I was placed in special classes and never once given the opportunity to see a therapist or any tools to help with my disorder. So naturally, I found other ways to self-soothe. Thinking back to those days doesn't fill me with joy, but it does remind me how far mental health practices have come. I would have given my first-born child for a widget spinner in elementary.

A good rule of thumb when it comes to being proactive with your mental state is to recognize when your mental health takes a turn for the worst, or you feel like you may be slipping backward. If you have emotional trauma in the form of undiagnosed bipolar or anxiety, you might feel a shift in the way you perceive information. One day you may look forward to brunch with the girls, and the next, you might dread such interactions. This should be the first clue of mental downfall, but there are others varying between how you see yourself in the mirror to worries about how other people see you. These are all examples of declining mental health and should be addressed as quickly as you can. If nothing else, go back over the steps of how to change your genetic make-up and return to that version of yourself. I am fully aware of the significance of self-care during times of depression and anxiety, so go easy on yourself. When all hope is lost, and you cannot see past the darkness, remember this:

Light is not what leads you out of dark places. It is courage. The courage to depend on your sense of hearing and your sense of touch; you can hear your mother's voice saying how proud she is of the person you've become, and you can feel generations of people holding your hand through the tough times and your head above water during the worst times.

Chapter 20: The Golden Gossip Girls

"Words have no wings, but they can fly a thousand miles."

— Korean proverb

Have you ever heard the phrase "Stay quiet, and your name can be heard on the breeze?" No? You couldn't have because I made it up. When I was a kid, I fit more comfortably under my grandmother's kitchen table than in a chair. I heard all kinds of things, from the weather forecast to Aunt Bonnie's cancer scare. I was up on current events in and out of my neighborhood and even how attracted one coffee mate was to President Clinton even after the whole Monica scandal.

At one point in my life, I honestly believed that coffee held powers harnessed from Columbia, derived from a mysterious clan of witches out of the Meddler district, and my grandma was their mystical leader. The tell-all, know-all, and wrangler of chatterboxes. If Pam down the street owed the furniture store fifteen dollars from last month's partial payment, it's because Bob can't keep up with the poker table and keeps coming home one more game away from the poor house. Speaking of the "poor house," Darlene found out the hard way that food stamps can't pay court costs and is now under federal investigation for food stamp misuse, and we all have to help her kids next week when the church offering comes around.

Fun fact: The poor house isn't actually a place; rather, it's a social status. I learned that one the hard way. The Salvation Army, while it possessed every characteristic of my Nana Ray's recent account, doesn't exactly care to be called that. And I'll go ahead and quote myself on this one for full transparency because credibility is important when taking advice from someone who knows what they're talking about, rather than someone who pretends to know what they are talking about. "Where lazy people go to eat when getting a job isn't exactly their cup of tea or cup of whisk-tea." Said while holding a ladle of beef stew one Sunday morning when Pastor Whatever asked me what this place means to me. Needless to say, I spent the next few Sundays at home writing that we don't make judgments on the needs of other people; only God can do that. To which I replied, well, can someone please tell Grandma she isn't God either? And now I can't eat pop-tarts in the kitchen and never figured out why Mary's daughter looked like Principal Daniels.

I had added a lot of humiliating stories to the list of things miscommunication had ruined for my family and me; in particular my Grandma Jean, who frequently got the raw end of the deal when something she said in the confidence of loose friends over an even looser bridge parties came back to bite her when exposed by the rumor mill. Might I add that if these are mere defamation phrases and not meant to be taken literally by a child who doesn't know what the word literally is, why name them like streets or public buildings? So, when I heard clothesline and grapevine, I didn't spend most of my investigative time posted up beside these points of access waiting to hear what kind of "situation" my cousin Kim found herself in after her boyfriend skipped town? Guess I'll never know.

While gossip can be entertaining and informative, it's not likely to get your likability rating up when it comes to being a credible friend. Like I said before, if they say it to you, they will say it about you. Rumors are like tall tales for red ears and uneducated housewives from the 1950s whose only other form of noteworthy information came in the form of a front porch swing.

The moral of the story is always what you are supposed to have learned. Don't let the cliff notes of something you heard in a rumor or gossip chain decide what people have learned from you. It comes down to nothing more than common sense. If you didn't hear it from the person who lived it, don't devise a story about it. That's the author's job. Speaking of authors, they are the first known source of gossip in history. Storytellers are brilliant. They draw you in with a subject you can visualize, like my grandmother's kitchen full of smoke rings. I would pop in with my number two pencil while taking notes on the journalist pad my dear old grandma got me for Christmas last year. The irony is spectacular. I know, as did my grandma, the minute she found it under the broken chair in her beauty shop and finally caught the blabbermouth that kept setting her up. While watching my handiwork go up in flames in the barbecue pit, I finally understood what telling on the storyteller was and never eavesdropped on my grandma again.

So, I began my first investigative reporter job, as unofficial editor Grandma Jean of course. Those nosey little parrots stood no chance against me on the scene reporting. Even though inquiring minds have always wanted to know, gossip can be dangerous and hurtful. When someone learned that someone else spoke about a private matter in a satirical tone, they feel like a joke, and rightly so. Who wants their marriage to be put under a scope because you saw something you thought was inappropriate when in reality it was chivalrous; then you tell a trusted friend in a highly confidential conversation your thoughts. Then that friend tells their "trusted" friend whatever their opinion was on the subject, that may or may not have been the same as yours, and so on and so on.

This begins something known as a "Whispering Campaign," and these types of gossip chains brought down the United States government without even knowing it. Insert the infamous Watergate scandal that disgraced several long-seated politicians, along with federal officers, and prompted the House of Representatives to start the second impeachment trial in U.S history. Followed by something that had never happened before in our over one hundred and eighty years of government: the first presidential resignation.

And to think, it is widely believed the tip came from a cheeky gossip chain who casually surrounded a water cooler during work breaks. Enter a new generation of gossip gals called "Water Cooler Talk." On the next episode, Gary decides Bob knows something about a file and connects it to a peculiar night where he saw a rummaging flashlight across the courtyard from his top-floor office that seemed to be looking for something in a chaotic fashion. And down goes the great wall of whatever faith was left in the United States government after the Vietnam War, which wasn't a lot to begin with. Sprinkle in FBI corruption and a national cover-up, and you've got to wonder just how many investigative reporters' heads spontaneously exploded that night.

The follow-up is going to come off as rhetorical, but I'd like you to consider these questions the next time the itch of interpersonal verbosity threatens irreparable hits to your character's integrity.

1. Did I hear it from the source?

2. Did I understand the information?

3. Is the person relaying the information credible?

If the answer is no to any of the questions above, abort the knowledge and carry on about your day. And get you some water. Contrary to popular belief, the water cooler isn't the stool pigeon the ears and mouths of nitwits are.

Part Three

Throughout one's life, you will inevitably meet five different types of personalities. These personality traits are known in the world of psychology as the Big Five. In 1949, D.W. Fiske began researching personalities and human traits. Since then, the evolution of what makes people who they have become is the backbone of human nature.

Personalities are second to fingerprints; the only difference between the two is you can't alter one, but the other can be modified with therapy and self-realization. Self-realization isn't as easy to accomplish as it sounds. Imagine you are a paleontologist exhuming the soft, brittle bones of a stegosaurus. You wouldn't dig with a machine; you would dig with small tools and brushes to avoid destroying that important piece of history. The same goes for your psyche; if you plow to the root, you're destroying the path it took you to get there, and ultimately the reward.

One of the most upsetting feelings a person can have is not understanding why someone doesn't like them. I've experienced plenty of situations where friends and partners didn't work out, and I was left feeling unwanted and self-conscious about what it was that I did to prevent a connection. The reality is, it wasn't technically something I did or didn't do; it was more about clashing personalities.

Let's take a look at the Big Five and uncover what kind of personality you connect with the most; this will give you an idea of how others perceive you and maybe answer some of those burning questions about why it didn't work out.

Chapter 21: The Big Five

"You cannot change what you are, only what you do."

— Philip Pullman

Openness

This trait features characteristics such as imagination and creativity. People who possess this trait also tend to have a broad range of interests. They are often referred to as multipotentiality. These types of people have trouble finding their "one true purpose" in life. They often feel they have many paths in life and attempt to pursue all of them. They are curious about the world and other people and eager to learn new things and enjoy new experiences. I like to call them the "Indiana Joneses" of the world.

Conscientiousness

This trait includes high levels of thoughtfulness, good impulse control, and goal-driven behaviors. Highly conscientious people are often organized and mindful of details. They plan ahead, think about how their behavior affects others, and are mindful of deadlines. These types of people tend to feel comfortable in leadership roles, such as teachers, managers, and CEO. If we didn't have these masters of success, the world would eventually fall into chaos, so if you see one or are one, pat yourself on the back for being the gorilla glue of our society.

Extraversion

Extraversion (or extroversion) is characterized by excitability, sociability, talkativeness, assertiveness, and high amounts of emotional expressiveness.People who are high in extraversion are outgoing and tend to gain energy in social situations. As the polar opposite of the wallflower, these personalities need to be around other people; this helps them feel alive and excited. Extroverts never seem to wind all the way down, and most of the time, they don't want to. You can thank these types of people for a great night out!

People who are low in extraversion (or introverted) tend to be more reserved and have less energy to expend in social settings. Introverted personalities are not so anti-social but more likely the quiet friend who doesn't want to karaoke but doesn't mind watching everyone else do so. Social events can feel draining to introverts and often require a period of solitude and quiet in order to "recharge."

Agreeableness

This personality trait includes attributes such as trust, kindness, affection, and other prosocial behaviors. People who are high in agreeableness tend to be more cooperative, while those on the low end of this trait tend to be more competitive and sometimes even manipulative. Always be mindful of the friend who agrees with everything, even if it involves negative backlash. You know, the friend that's like "Yeah, it's a good idea to jump off the roof" after six cocktails. I guess everything is a good idea when you're not the one breaking your ankle at 3 am.

Neuroticism

Neuroticism is a trait characterized by sadness, moodiness, and emotional instability. Everyone knows this trait and this person. This is the friend who only calls to complain about what's bothering them. These people seem to have a black cloud hovering over them and get offended easily, causing a stir in the positive aura pot of conversation. Individuals who are high in this trait tend to experience mood swings, anxiety, irritability, and sadness. I call them the "Charlie Browns" of the world; others might refer to them as Negative Nancy's or the newest member of the neurotic roster "The Karen."

Have you found your personality trait yet? I'm sure it doesn't come as a surprise to most. And you might be asking if these traits can be universal? And the answer to that question is: absolutely. In the past fifty years of this theory, these personality traits have been tried and tested in virtually every culture on the planet and reached the same conclusion every time.

Based on this extensive research, many psychologists now believe that the five personality dimensions are not only universal; they also have biological origins. Psychologist David Buss has proposed an evolutionary explanation for these five core personality traits, suggesting that these exact personality traits represent the most important qualities that shape our social landscape. This suggests the Big Five and how you may have developed your trait is based on environmental data. In layman's terms, it means how and where you were raised.

Take, for example, the nature vs. nurture debate. This theory suggests that human behavior is determined by the environment vs. by their genes. It's been used since medieval times in defense of natural-born royalty. The research behind this states that people who weren't in a specific bloodline couldn't possibly understand nor pursue the battle trait or reproductive traits of their ancestors. The end result being inbreeding and exclusion. It's no wonder they were all perpetually plagued by disease and general depression and anxiety. I mean, they were a product of an environment that was solely based around survival, leaving no room for happiness or even normalcy.

Nature is a general pre-wiring of the human mind. These are traits that are influenced by genetic inheritance and other biological factors. At the same time, nurture is generally what type of emotional environment you are raised in. It is believed that if you are raised in a traumatic or dangerous environment, you often develop Neuroticism or Conscientiousness. The reason behind this is a need to bring order to the world. But on the other hand, scientists believe that trauma could be a genetic trait passed down from generations, causing someone to become just like their pre-wired predecessors.

As confusing as all of that might be, I ask you this. How were you raised? Do you find that your distinct personality is more like your mother or more of a testament to how your mother raised you? Some people use the environment they were raised in as a scapegoat for the environment they create as adults. If you are someone who says "I can't help it, that's just the way I was raised" as an excuse for bad behaviors, you might find it helpful to examine how you grew up versus you as a grown-up.

An example of self-realization is understanding that what you've been through isn't an excuse to prevent you from becoming who you can be, because the root of self-realization is fulfilling one's true potential. So how can a person discover who they are and who they want to be if they constantly hide behind trauma or denial?

Whether you believe in therapy or not, you must open yourself up to the possibility that your personality is a choice on some level. I used to know this girl in college who came from a bad neighborhood. Her parents were abusive and criminals. For years, I knew this young lady, and not for one moment did I ever suspect that she had ever gone through something traumatic in her life. She wore the sincerest smile every time I saw her and offered to help any chance she got. Her personality was similar to openness but also agreeableness. By combining the two traits, she successfully eliminated the chance of becoming anything like her environment.

When I asked her how she could wire herself so well and make it seem believable, she replied "Because it's not a lie, it's not who I pretend to be. It's who I am." Confused, I asked "But you've been through a lot, most people couldn't even imagine the…" she kindly cut me off and said, "If you had a choice to be rain or a rainbow, which would you choose?" I responded with, "Rainbow, of course." And then she said, "What I went through doesn't have to affect my future because, like all hurtful things, I let it die a long time ago."

This made me think. If a flower is watered every day, it will remain alive. Could the same concept be used for an emotional childhood or any kind of trauma, for that matter? If you continue to water memory or stress, it will continue to thrive; but if you stop watering it, eventually you'll be able to throw the empty pot into the trash. In the years since knowing that little self-proclaimed rainbow, I have met more and more people who have decided to kill every plant they can. And by doing so, they live happier and more successful lives than people who live in a manifested garden of despair and defeat.

The Big Five may give you an idea of how many plants you have been watering and how it's affecting your adult relationships and your personal growth. Use your findings to check your behavior at the door because, as terrible as it may sound, human beings only react to things they understand. So, most won't accurately understand something that happened to you because it didn't happen to them. It's a classic case of you had to be there. And they weren't, so don't expect someone you just met or have known forever to understand why you are the way you are because that's not their job. It's your job to find your rainbow, and that starts by drying up the rain.

Chapter 22: The Myers-Briggs Type Indicator

"Equals Quasi Scientific Jargon"

— me

Another "tool" or "childish parlor game" to determine your personality is a model called the Myers-Briggs Type Indicator.

The Myers-Briggs Type Indicator (MBTI) is an introspective self-report, multiple-choice questionnaire that is said to indicate differing personalities and how they choose to see and respond to the world around them. The Myers-Briggs test wasn't developed by middle-aged white men with PhDs like the Big Five. It was actually developed long before the Big Five in 1917 by Katharine Cook Briggs.

Katharine began her research into personalities after the birth of her third child, and only child to survive past infancy, her daughter Isabel Briggs-Myers. Mrs. Briggs did something remarkable and unheard of at the time. She set up a research lab inside of her home to observe her infant daughter's personality traits and the way she responded and reacted to the world around her, especially the environment of which her mother had created.

Brigg's theory was originally based on the conceptual theory proposed by Swiss psychiatrist Carl Jung. Jung speculated that people experience the world using four psychological functions: Intuition, Sensation, Feeling, and Thinking. He also proclaimed that one of these functions is dominant for a person all of their life. Meaning he believed that every human on earth is born with a specific personality code and will die with that same code. According to the MBTI, there are four different categories under which one can fall.

Introversion/Extroversion: The quality of being shy and reticent vs. outgoing and overly expressive.

Sensing/Intuition: Perceives by sense or senses vs. the ability to understand something immediately without the need for conscious reasoning.

Thinking/Feeling: The process of using one's mind to consider or reason about something vs. an emotional state or reaction.

Judging/Perceiving: A form of opinion or conclusion without context vs. becoming aware or conscious of something; coming to realize or understand.

After extensively studying the English version of Carl Jung's book of Psychological Types, Katharine Briggs developed a typology wherein she proposed four temperaments of human behavior in an attempt to turn Jung's theory of psychological types to practical use. Once Isabel graduated from Swarthmore College in 1919, she joined her mother's ideology and decided to help manage psychometric testing for her mother and make it accessible to the masses.

Fun Fact: Neither one of these two women had any formal education in the field of psychology. Like, zero. Whatever claims they made were just that, experience-based claims and held absolutely no scientific basis. So, how did this test become the world's first and favorite psychological test?

During World War II, this mother-daughter pair decided to market the test as an indicator of personality preferences in the workforce. Briggs and Myers sought to identify workers who fit the description for a particular workplace environment. This type of indicator test would allow hirers to identify workers who were "the most comfortable and effective" for company duties. It was also the beginning of preconceived discrimination in the workplace. Every person has a preconceived self-image and notions of their own strengths and weaknesses, making it impossible to get accurate data from individuals who are self-typecast. Meaning people who "think" they are helpful, when in reality, they buckle under pressure.

Confidence is a double-edged sword in this case. Overconfidence could have you answering questions in a predictive tone or hypothetically themed. For instance, one of the questions in the test is "Do you get bored easily if there isn't a task to complete?" I wouldn't answer no; that would be silly. Predictively speaking, I would be crawling up the walls of my cubical or behind a cash register in ADHD desperation. But hypothetically, I would say it would be possible for me to adapt to the environment.

With the help of Donald W. MacKinnon, the head of the Institute of Personality and Social Research, the mother-daughter team published the first edition of the Myers-Briggs Type Indicator test; and the rest is well, history.

The Myers-Briggs Personality Type Matrix:

Introvert Variables:

ISTJ: Responsible, sincere, analytical, reserved, hardworking with sound practical judgment.

ISFJ: Warm, considerate, responsible, pragmatic, and thorough. Caretakers who enjoy being helpful to others.

INFJ: Idealistic, organized, insightful, dependable, and gentle. Intellectual harmony seekers.

INTJ: Innovative, independent, strategic, logical. Driven by their own ideas for improvement.

ISTP: Action-oriented, logical, spontaneous, independent. Action seekers, mechanically skilled at understanding how things work.

ISFP: Gentle, sensitive, helpful, flexible. Enjoys practical aesthetics, especially in the workplace.

INFP: Creative, adaptable, loyal, idealistic. Values inner harmony and personal growth.

INTP: Imaginative, reserved, precise, and flexible. Original thinkers who enjoy creative problem-solving.

Extrovert Variables:

ESTP: Outgoing, action-oriented, and curious. Pragmatic problem solvers and skillful negotiators.

ESFP: Playful, enthusiastic, friendly, and tactful. Possess strong common sense and a helpful nature.

ENFP: Optimistic, supportive, playful, and spontaneous. Value inspiration and enjoy starting new projects.

ENTP: Inventive, strategic, enterprising, and inquisitive. Enjoys a challenge and new ideas.

ESTJ: Outgoing, analytical, efficient, and dependable. Likes to run the show and get things done in an orderly fashion.

ESFJ: Conscientious, reliable, productive, and organized. People pleasers who love being active.

ENFJ: Diplomatic, idealistic, responsible, and caring. Skilled communicators who value deeper connections.

ENTJ: Strategic, logical, outgoing, and ambitious. Effective organizers and long-range planners.

As you can see, the personality types are pretty vague in nature; most of the Introverts are similar invariants, and the Extroverts are as well. Depending on the multiple-choice answer, you choose how these codes are produced and then tattooed across your forehead, assumably preventing any option for change.

The idea of this test is to reveal personality traits your brain is hiding or has hidden from you. The result is figuring out what makes you tick and how you relate to the world around you. This can open the door for understanding all parts of you instead of lies you have unknowingly told yourself. Imagine a situation where you aren't chosen for a particular job due to your introvert nature, because the job responsibilities require an outgoing personality. Does that seem fair? No, it doesn't; here's why.

Extroverted people, while they may be more excitable and entertaining, doesn't mean they can do a job better than someone who is not so outgoing. Correct me if I am wrong, but normally in an interview situation, when a person is asked if they can practice patience and professionalism, it is likely that both personalities would say "Yes." This is because everyone, no matter what, rolls out of bed in the morning and puts their pants on the same way. Far be it for an introvert to be judged in a work environment, simply because they are quieter and more reserved than an extrovert. Do you see my point? The difference between the two parties is nothing more than a personal preference that isn't even based upon what you will do at work, but rather the way you operate in theory. The word theory is used very loosely here because everyone is capable of modifying behavior to suit the needs of an employer. Here's a theory that isn't considered: judging a book by its cover or personality code would be a little counterproductive and biased if you ask me.

From a psychological standpoint, I see what Myers and Briggs were trying to accomplish. They intended to create a universal "matrix" to determine what kind of personalities enjoy certain things and which don't. This would open the door to becoming who you want to be or making what passions you aspire to more easily reachable. The Indicator could also be used for choosing life partners and even what job you would be good at based on a series of code-like numbers.

But the downfall of this pseudo-science is the lack of accurate scientific study and isolated variables. There are 16 different personality type codes, but who's to say there aren't more? Placing the human mind inside such a small box is not only dangerous but also unfair. If Eugenics has taught us anything, it is not to mess with nature. Determining a person's value based upon their desirable or undesirable characteristics is essentially "breeding out personality flaws" which is inhuman and absurd.

Overall, the Myers-Biggs results can be used to foster the understanding of the human perspective but shouldn't be used in a "people-picking" module and should be taken with a grain of salt.

Introverts unite and study in libraries and hole-in-the-wall bars. Extroverts charge those batteries at pool parties and social conferences. And the next time you are presented with a "personality test" when applying for a job, simply decline the offer because who would want to work for a clearly biased and exclusion-based company anyway?

If you would like to take the extensive Myers-Briggs personality type indicator, make sure you are taking the original version on the Myers-Briggs website. A lot of employers and Google savvy copycats have altered versions of the test that will give you false codes. Since the personality codes were never copyrighted by Myers, the use of these letters can be reproduced in any variation and called legitimate.

While the test is real and can give you a general idea of whether you are an introvert or extrovert, my guess is if the scientific backing of a fetal code is correct, then you probably already know which of the two you are. In conclusion, don't take this test so seriously; play around with the results and use them for self-discovery and change. Also, to discredit any prior discourse that involves the idea of permanent stamps succeeding your birth. We will leave that to horoscopes for now.

Chapter 23: The Finches

"It would be impossible to fix on any definite point where the term 'man' ought to be used."

— Charles Darwin

Throughout my many years of studying the human experience, I've come across a couple of resounding truths, one being that people are ever evolving. Darwin defined evolution as "descent with modification." Essentially, he believed species change over time, which creates new species that share a common ancestor. I've always oversimplified this theory with the takeaway being "only the strong survive." Darwin, while in the Galapagos Islands, found similar but nonidentical species of finches living in the same environment. He also noted that each individual finch species was well-suited for the environment and had a specific role. For instance, the size and strength of their claws and beaks varied. The species that ate large seeds tended to have large, tough beaks, compared to the finches that ate worms and other insects; they had thin, sharp beaks. What Darwin observed after returning to Europe was that the pattern of finches was similar to species on the nearby mainland of Ecuador but different from those found anywhere else in the world.

The point is, the finches on the island gradually adapted to local conditions over many generations and long periods of time, creating a blueprint of the formation of one or more distinct species on each island. This is called adaptation.

When we compare this theory to the human mind, we get the same result. Cultivating an adaptive mindset can be essential in the workplace or a resilient friendship. An adaptive mindset is a mindset assessing facts and circumstances of a situation, and then making certain adjustments to thrive in that particular environment or scenario. These brilliant creatures are known in the world of psychology as a social conversant. Just like the finch, they make the most of the moment, learning from mistakes and ultimately making necessary changes in order to survive and move forward. Evolution is changing, and just like the Galapagos finches, it happens over generations and a long period of time.

If you believe you grow from experiences and mistakes, you will also agree creative solutions are most likely the process. How well you bounce back from mistakes depends on your belief that intelligence and learning developed through a system of effort allows for the ability to improve through change. Experiences where you find yourself on the short end of the promotion stick, or that "left out" feeling when you just can't find anything to add to a conversation, can be a result of dormant obstinacy.

Mistakes and situations that leave you feeling uncomfortable or judged can actually be a perfect chance to become adaptive. You didn't get the promotion? Find out why and change it. If they say you weren't hungry enough or had attendance issues, the next day, show up like your social evolution depends on it. If they think you aren't hungry enough, show them how hungry you can be. Adapt to your environment through modifying your goals and behaviors.

Comedians always talk about becoming a student of your environment. Anyone can be funny, maybe not on stage, under hot lights being heckled funny, but funny in your own way. Pay close attention to what your friends or co-workers find funny, then go out and study whatever it was they laughed at. Trust me, the world is naturally comedic; just ask any New Yorker. It's not a case-by-case study; it's becoming a lifelong learner, opening yourself up to new experiences, and eventually, you will find relatability.

Adaption can be neglected throughout generations; this comes in the form of something called a "generational deficit." A good example of a generational deficit or curse would be an undiagnosed mental illness. Think about it. Four generations before you suffered from bipolar disorder, the first two generations presumably would have realized there was something off about their personality, but due to lack of mental health services, adapted ways to control it or remedy it with the tools they had at the time. After the Vietnam war, mental illness cases soared. So, the government implemented more research and testing, opening the floodgates for people suffering from things they couldn't explain, eventually ushering in a new era in mental health. Suddenly doctors were diagnosing anxiety, post-traumatic stress, and depression.

Finally, the generational curse can be lifted and treated, or so you would think. The way your ancestors dealt with the condition is ingrained into your DNA. Plenty of parents watched as their parents merely survived their undiagnosed ailments. This could come in the form of alcoholism or extreme dieting, or even abuse. This type of toxicity could lead to such disorders as addiction and self-mutilation in their offspring.

Generational curses will be and must be broken eventually; that's how family trees grow. Little by little, these ancestral burdens fall away by implementing change. Remember, don't allow too much space for skeletons that don't belong to you. If your dad was a drug addict and so was his dad, instead of following their misfortune, you have a chance to break that curse. But to do that, you must make the necessary adjustments.

If you're not sure how or when to change, here is a model to outline the steps.

The Five Steps of Change

Precontemplation: The first step isn't a step at all; it's active denial. It is the act of realizing there is a problem and intentionally ignoring it. Similar to the phrase "Ignore the problem, and hope it goes away." I assure you; high functioning mental illness is not something you can sweep under the rug; well, at least not anymore. It's highly intrusive and, with today's medicines/therapy, unbelievably easy to treat. The enemy of change is stubbornness—break that generational curse and choose to get on to step two.

Contemplation: Discover when and where the problem began and how other family members attempted to soothe or control the issue. Suppose your grandmother was a negative person; that most likely bled over to your father, who eventually caused your social anxiety and/or negative coping skills. You are now aware of what needs to be changed and are ready to move on in a healthier way.

Preparation: Just like when preparing to move, you must pack up some of your issues and remove obstacles from your path in order to move forward successfully. Before you move, you must get ready to do so. You wouldn't throw everything you own into a trash bag and hit the road, would you? No, you would formulate a system or list of things to do, like calling a U-Haul service and gathering boxes and tape. At the very least, buy bubble wrap to protect your things from breaking. The same goes for preparing to change; you need to have a realistic plan, so none of your other priceless talents are affected. You wouldn't want to lose your sense of humor while wrapped up in your inability to change your social anxiety. Use your sense of humor as a way to combat said social anxiety by gradually tweaking the way you react to things like blind dates or small dinner parties. Have a couple of clever stories and funny anecdotes on deck to ease distressing situations.

Action: Once you have identified what needs fixing or change, this is the call to action. Take everything you have learned from your family's background and intel from your childhood, and steer toward the other side of the road. This can be a long process of trial and error, but persistence is the only way to achieve genuine transformation. If it gets tough and you quit, then the curse will inevitably be passed on; action and dedication will make sure your family's vexation ends with you.

Maintenance: Once you've conquered and wiped out the plaque that threatens the growth of your family tree, maintain the change. Just like flowers need insecticides to keep ladybugs from drilling tiny holes in their leaves, the branches of your tree need conservation to survive and flourish. This comes in the form of continuous care. Once you've defeated the ladybug, that doesn't mean there aren't a thousand ladybugs ready to test your remedy.

You are steadfast and capable; you were born with the ability to evolve as a person. Your parents didn't look at you the day you were born and think "This child will be just like me." Far from it, most parents live by the rule of betterment "This child will be the future of this family." While it may seem like a vague statement because literally everyone born into a bloodline is the future, not everyone has the capability to crack generational obstinacy in half. Show them procreated bullheadedness can be used for good, not evil.

Chapter 24: Practice Forgiveness

"Forgiveness is the key to action and freedom."

— Hannah Arendt

As most of us grow and change, one act we don't commonly exercise is the act of forgiveness. When you make positive changes, you have to consider forgiving yourself for your past transgressions. As merciful as it may seem to forgive others for their wrongdoings, you should be as generous to yourself. When I found myself on the wrong side of the tracks in my early twenties, I made some mistakes that directly affected the people closest to me. During my adult transformation, I apologized to some of the people I hurt. What I didn't realize was I never really apologized to myself, which left underlying resentment toward the person I used to be.

Changing who you are or repairing the damage you've caused to yourself isn't something someone thinks about when they are in the process of healing. The word change is pretty straightforward; it means to make something different. Like I said, pretty clear cut. Someone could get this definition confused with replaced or swapped, which suggests the original remains in some capacity. This is simply not the case. You are transforming what was to what is, and there is power in recognizing the true nature of who you will or have become. This starts with forgiveness and letting go of the cinder blocks attached to your ankle; the blocks of contradiction that, no matter how hard you try to stay above water, keep dragging you under. I had a couple of cinder blocks and plenty of fish that couldn't wait for me to give up and become their nourishment.

Once I realized failure was a part of learning, I began to ease up on myself and began carrying scissors. Every time the sting of past disappointment would rear its ugly head, I would reach beneath the rising tide and cut it loose. I would then explain to the new me that the old me didn't understand healthy boundaries. I would silently apologize to the new me for the old me's attempt to derail our extensive progress and quickly move on from the weight that memory held.

Of course, that's not to say that is the last time a memory would try and drown me. I'm just saying pessimistic memories don't have to hold so much power. I am hesitant to use the phrase "mind over matter," and trust me, I am using it lightly here. But for the sake of explanation, I will say if ever you are faced with a vociferous skeleton who just refuses to stay buried, plan a vacation for it. Okay, stay with me here.

Invite your chatty skeleton to Colorado. When you get there, take a hike; when you reach the top of the highest mountain, throw that garrulous skeleton off, then mindfully watch as it scatters with every impact. Then be done with it; there is zero chance you can change its point of view because the only point of view it's capable of is the past, and you are not defined by your past. Mind over matter isn't a magic trick. It's the nature of victory. Victory over those cinder blocks and skeletons and victory over hungry fish, just waiting for you to fail.

No one wants to be fish food, but that doesn't mean you won't be. Everyone fails. Eventually, it's ingrained into our species. Some of the most successful people in the world not only failed, but failed several times before becoming successful. It's natural to want to prove people wrong or impress them, but perfect people don't exist, so don't try to be one. It's also natural to disappoint yourself, and when you do, try to stay optimistic.

Forgiveness is a gift, like the ability to fix something that's broken without knowing how it was put together in the first place. The practice of forgiving doesn't have a particular focus. It is used to recover all things. A friendship, a parent, or yourself; it makes no difference, really. As long as you are forgiving, you are restoring positivity and creating a constructive atmosphere for personal and interpersonal growth.

Go ahead and say "I'm sorry." Trust me; it feels better than you would think.

Chapter 25: Complete Joy

"I've learned that people will forget what you said, people will forget what you did, but people will never forget how you made them feel."

— Maya Angelou

One of the many wonders of the world happens to be inspirational people. You know, the kind of people who can turn devastation into encouragement and problems into incentives. I have a friend who fits this description so well I often refer to her as "Jubilant Joy." It works out pretty well on account of her actual name is Joy. Now, Joy isn't a product of her environment by any means. She, like the little college rainbow I told you about earlier, decided she was going to triumph in the face of adversity.

Joy grew up in the deep south; she was raised by callus parents who would accept nothing but success and the ability to teach and carry-on traditions. When Joy realized she was being raised by narcissistic parents and surrounded by a slew of negative, self-absorbed family members, she formulated a plan. She knew at a certain age she would be able to escape the sinking ship she was trapped on. But to do that, she would need some life rafts, a whistle, and plenty of clean water and sustainable food. She knew she would be floating around for some time before she found dry land; this land came in the form of higher education. But long before that, she was steadily gathering the tools needed to jump ship safely; but what were the tools exactly?

The life rafts: Figuratively speaking, these would be her unwavering perseverance, diligence, and sheer will to remove herself from the environment.

The whistle: This tool would be her intelligence and her ability to use valuable resources like her imagination and problem-solving skills.

Reserve of food & water: This would most certainly be defined as her stamina and spiritual resilience.

Without this internal support system, she would have failed in her attempt to resist her family's generational pull. It's been proven time after time when a person doesn't like the habitat they are in, rarely does that spark change. What it does is create a biosphere of complaints and/or general indifference. Have you ever heard anyone say "I live in an asphalt jungle, but my heart belongs to the beach?" Or some other nonsensical reasoning like "It's just who we are, and how we were raised; why would I question what I have been taught by my parents?" These are generational roadblocks and domains of forced acceptance.

Joy saw these roadblocks and challenged every single one of them. So, when the time came for her to jump into the choppy waters of uncertainty, she was certain she would survive. She knew what it meant to stay sanctioned aboard her family's descending ship; it meant she too would become a damaged ship bobbing up and down in the ocean.

Since then, Joy has inspired and helped others find their own way out of dangerous and rough waters. Her tenacity and bewitching nature, I'm sure, is what keeps her on the path of righteousness. I also know there is a bit of charisma that can only come from survival; after all, intense pressure and stress are the only way to create a diamond.

Diamonds are one of the most beautiful gifts this rotating space ball can produce, so we endlessly search for them. It has been said that we as a human race will do anything to find riches in dark places; why is it that we covet things that can bring temporary substance, instead of people who have a natural ability to turn hardship into prosperity? Or the ability to uncover a diamond in the rough, reminding the diamond there is another place to shine without the rough; therefore, allowing the hidden gem to be seen as what it was meant to be—a sparkling example of redemption.

Joy and other people just like her don't have a gift or even a talent for what they do. Being inspirational isn't something you are born with, quite the opposite, really. Inspiring people are people who choose to see the world from a different angle. You and I might see the rain falling and get mildly upset, wondering when it will stop so we don't get wet on our way out the door. Poignant people will see the rain and understand that flowers need water to grow and worry less about getting wet than finding the rainbow, which will undoubtedly follow the storm.

I can say it until I am blue in the face and will always get this response. "So, because I don't like the winter, does that make me uninspired and negative?" I will always reiterate that not enjoying something isn't an uninspiring trait, although how you react to it is. Everyone finds winter unappealing, but not everyone complains about it every day or allows it to determine what kind of mood they are in. That is toxic negativity, which we will cover a little later.

Everything comes down to happiness in the end. High spirits will always be inspirational because they are few and far between in the world we live in. To become inspirational, you have to have the ability to find happiness and convey that benevolence in conversations and social situations. I've never seen Joy waiver from her compassionate mission; she doesn't fake her generosity. It's the truest thing about her. If you are planning on being kind just to see if it makes you appear charming, don't. I can promise you if it's not sincere, you could be setting yourself up for presumption and condescension, two traits you do not want to be compared to. Instead, consider setting a quota at the beginning of your journey to joy.

Each day give yourself a quota to meet; this can be how many strangers you smile at or engage in conversation throughout the day. Or how many positive messages you will send to friends and family, creating surprise cheer which sets up a happiness chain that, for all you know, could go on for days, even years. Random acts of kindness are fortunate interactions and have a way of accidentally creating an advantageous atmosphere that breeds positivity and compassion even if you're not there to reap the benefits.

My mother used to always tell my siblings and I that a great act of kindness is like shining a light into the darkness. You have an idea of who can see the light on the other side; you can only truly see from where you are standing. So never think your light cannot be seen; when you are kind to someone, your light shines on through their eyes. The end result is infinite light, one that travels further than your feet could ever imagine.

Here are some acts of kindness you can do every day to meet your inspirational quota.

1. Tell a stranger you like something they are wearing or a book they are carrying. Don't be afraid to induce a conversation; this is what we as a society are most lacking.

2. Send out handwritten letters or holiday cards to people that may not be involved with your inner circle. Denounce exclusivity; it serves no one. This isn't 1955, and you are not making a guest list for your bridge party. Invite everyone; that's how new friendships are made.

3. Make a list of charitable events and show up to as many as you can. You don't always have to get your hands dirty cleaning elderly people's gutters or volunteering at homeless shelters. Although these are the types of foundations that stay in dire need of helpers, so try and be available for those things. You can also donate food and clothing to places like The Salvation Army.

4. Tell one person a day what they mean to you, and yes, this counts for yourself. If you can't find someone or run out of people who make your life happy, then tell yourself how you bring joy to the space around you.

Trust the process and open your heart to kindness. They say a smile is more contagious than a yawn, and they (whoever "they" are) would be right. There has never been a time where someone has smiled at me in passing, and I deliberately denied returning the warmness. Not one single time. Thanks, Joy.

Chapter 26: How Attractive is Your Character?

"Beauty gets the attention; personality gets the heart."

-Unknown

There will always be a link between personality and beauty. The link is obvious; if you're pretty on the inside, you will become beautiful on the outside as well. The standard for beauty has long since been misconstrued as the perfect combination of physical traits. Blonde hair, blue eyes being two of the "perfect" traits of attractiveness. The idea of captivating beauty is a "package deal" and far more complicated than what color eyes you do or don't have. We've all experienced the proclamation heard round the world, "She is the whole package!" The idea behind this exciting declaration is that a person has found inner beauty as well as outer beauty, along with complementary talents and traits that seem to come delicately wrapped and sealed with a bow.

What does this package actually look like? If you are looking to widen your audience of admirers, I have refined a list of qualities and personality traits that could possibly assist your descent into your own beautiful package; and if you work toward these additional personality perks, you will effortlessly tie your bow up neatly.

Three Personality Traits That Make You Instantly More Attractive

1. A positive attitude: Do you see a pattern of positivity? If I haven't said it enough in this book, "A positive outlook and attitude is like opening the front door of a restaurant for the dinner rush. You have the ability to welcome people without saying a word." Optimism has been revealed as one of the most common attributes mentioned in surveys about attractive qualities and dating. This answer was the same for both sexes.

2. Balanced extroversion: A balanced extrovert will help you appear fresh in social situations. Full-blown extroverts tend to live outside most boxes; they don't tire easily and prefer being around people far more often than social constraints allow. If you went to a blowout party on Friday, try and just have dinner with a few friends or spouse on Saturday. Extreme extroverts tend to overstay their welcome. Find a balance between too much and not enough, and you will become someone everyone looks forward to seeing.

3. Confidence: Confidence, again, is not to be confused with arrogance. Being overconfident is just as bad as having none at all—practice speaking with conviction and allowing for vulnerability. Think too highly of yourself, and others will notice; think of yourself conservatively, with a bit of poise.

This allows for assurance in your unique talents, and if you asked me, that's why confidence has been the most attractive quality since surveys were invented. People just gravitate toward individuals who are comfortable in their own skin.

There's no rule book when it comes to knowing what people find appealing in a partner. The fact is, if you asked 10 women and 10 men what they found most attractive in a partner, you might be surprised by some of the answers. I did this exact survey for this book. Let's find out what my scientific study revealed.

When I asked 20 adults over the age of 21 respectively, what three qualities are more desirable when looking for in a potential partner, the results were sort of a mixed bag and one of the guys clearly misunderstood the invitation to survey. He kept mixing up the word qualities and bodily. Yeesh.

Question One: What is the first thing you observe when speaking to someone new?

a. Posture

b. The way they speak

c. Ability to use eye contact

Eight out of 10 women chose eye contact, and seven out of 10 men agreed. Except for Ryan, who said "A girl's eyes have to be pretty." Unbelievable.

Question Two: When speaking to a potential partner, what is more important?

a. A sense of humor

b. A sense of comfort

c. A sense of intelligence

This question was intense because when we think of the whole package, all of these traits are necessary. I assured the crowd that I wasn't trying to degrade any of these traits or remove them. I am simply asking which one would come first.

Ryan was quickly omitted from this question because he replied comfortably, as in "Big boobs are super comfortable when napping." I think I can tell who the "funny one" is in this group, and I oddly respected him for it. The answers included five women who said a sense of humor, three women who said a sense of comfort, and two women who said a sense of intelligence.

On the male side, four men said a sense of comfort while the other five men said a sense of humor.

This continued for several more questions and ended with the most important question of them all. What is in your package? What do you think you have in your box of exemplary traits?

Out of the 20 people, minus Ryan—he drank too many Long Island iced teas and was escorted out of the building before the dinner rush ended—the answers varied widely. This experiment was successful in narrowing down real-life expectations compared to overall expectations. In doing so, I discovered that it's a matter of personal preference; no one person likes the same qualities in a mate. The question of what you have in your package in my research is universal in the sense that everyone sort of gives you this look, a look of I don't know.

To one person, a sense of humor is the most attractive trait; to another, finding comfort in a warm personality feels right. Every human being on this earth has the ability to choose their own partner's present. It is every human's responsibility to accurately fill their personality box with honest character references; this alleviates the "I don't know" look.

But it would be good to note, when searching for the man or woman of your dreams, don't get caught up in what they present to you. This is a common mistake amongst the younger generation. The use of social media has single-handedly reduced the element of surprise; you don't have the option to learn mannerisms or posture or even the way they speak, void of preparation and without text.

Online dating is good for handpicking your package deal while picking up your dinner. But that package deal might not fare so well when it's actually delivered. Truth be told, anyone can claim to be funny, charming, and attractive when given the option to choose such attributes. If I were a part of the dating scene (heaven forbid), I would be tempted to say I was funny, outgoing, and just for the heck of it, I'd throw in that I am proficient in time management and capable of attaining optimal organization. The last two characteristics couldn't be further from who I am, but they sound fantastic. Taking into consideration that my neurodivergent brain would never allow such things as organization and being on time, it's a cruel joke, if anything. If I were to ever get serious with anyone, those last two claims would ultimately make a liar out of me, and most people will not tolerate bold-faced liars or even humor them when choosing a life partner.

Part Four

If you have ever belly laughed or swore you couldn't breathe after a joke, you know what it's like to feel pure joy. Here are some different types of comedy that just keep us coming back for more!

Spontaneous Humor:

This type of satire arises out of circumstance. Don't bother trying to rehearse spontaneous humor because it's just that, spontaneous. It only works in the moment, with those people, in that environment. This comes in the form of indirect humor, such as a flashing sign on the interstate saying "Road Work Ahead," and my teenage daughter said from the back seat "Well I would hope so." It took me a second to process her quick wit, but when I did, I spit my tea out onto my steering wheel in a fit of laughter. Spontaneous humor is mostly associated with comedic timing. Incorporating irony and logical thought is a recipe for unprompted quick and witty comedic timing.

Constructed Humor:

This is your typical stand-up comedy show. The comic you see on the stage has a carefully contrasted background and certain framework to his or her performance. The jokes have been practiced and tested amongst different individuals that would make up the demographic audience. Stand-up humor is loosely based on relationships and work environments or real-life topics that can be relatable to the average person. A comedic spin on these topics and observations into shock-provoking laughter creates a picture inside the minds of their audiences.

Chapter 27: The Art of Being Funny

"There's only one true superpower amongst human beings, and that is being funny. People treat you differently if you can make them laugh."

— Jeff Garlin

Intentional humor:

Intentional humor doesn't begin with an intent to say something funny but rather to say something obvious or clever in a stagnant environment to lighten the mood. This can range from a funny quip to poking fun at your surroundings or people in a charming way, not a ruthless or mean way.

Take one of my experiences, for example. My friend Samantha had a habit of controlling conversations by talking endlessly about her Tinder dates and how she doesn't understand why none of these guys are working out and that none of them look like their profile pictures. Intentional humor would sound something like this.

"Statistically speaking, 9 out of 10 of these profiles are made up of characters with pretty words and poor development skills and are bound to unravel right around the third date. So, keep it in your pants till then."

Sam replies "*But he has such a nice smile.*" To which I follow up with this quip gem "So did Ted Bundy, sis. So did Ted Bundy."

Comedic individuals often rely on their audience's associated and learned responses. These are called anchors. This is something I learned in a theatre somewhere between wanting to be a comic and a serious writer. I often found myself in the thralls of two separate worlds or what I thought was two separate worlds. It wasn't until I was given a chance to do an advice column with a local newspaper, did I understand how powerful, intelligent comedy can be.

Theatre was a necessary outlet I needed to pursue to maintain a sense of wonder and freedom during the stifling workload I carried early on in college. I obtained some serious scholarships through some promising literary agencies and had a pretty heavy workload to maintain these scholarships. So, I took a drama class and joined the local theater as a hobby three days a week.

While I learned a lot of different kinds of acting, my favorite kind was improvisation. Improv is loosely based upon anchors allowing the person to draw from jokes like "Why did the chicken cross the road?" You see, there can be an infinite number of reasons why a chicken would want to cross the road. But everyone knows the answer is "To get to the other side." That is an anchor; it's an associated and learned response. Although it was funny as a child, it isn't so funny as an adult. Most of the time, if the anchor is switched to something relatable like "because it would rather risk getting hit by a car than to return home to its fat chicken wife and bad chicken kids," you would laugh at the joke because it is familiar in tone and because you expected the comic to bring it back to life in a fresh and relatable way. This is knowledge-based humor that transcends cultures and creates a type of historic laughter. Historic laughter is sort of a blueprint for comedians.

Jerry Seinfeld is one of the greatest comedians the world has ever known. As far as observations go, he is king, drawing from simple situations and the world he lives in. He also relies on anchors; subjects he knows have historically proven to get a laugh. Here is a great example of historical laughter and the use of an anchor.

"I'll tell you what I like about Chinese people. They're hanging in there with the chopsticks, aren't they? You know they've seen the fork. They're staying with the sticks. I'm impressed by that. I don't know how they missed it. A Chinese farmer gets up, works in the field with the shovel all day... Shovel... Spoon... Come on... There it is. You're not plowing 40 acres with a couple of pool cues..." – Jerry Seinfeld.

Okay, pop quiz: Why is that funny? It's funny because it's true. It's a classic observation of the Chinese culture and has proven time and time again to make people laugh.

When I was a theater student, I wanted to be like Jerry but came off more like Kevin James in the sense of his nature is more slapstick and self-deprecating. I had a knack for making fun of myself and using my body as a tool in doing so. I often talked with my hands and fell down for laughs. The end result was most of the laughter was at me and not so much with me.

Throughout my years of writing, I've developed a comedic undertone that is all my own. But it didn't happen overnight; I had to work at it. I would take on side projects that enhanced my comedic writing, such as writing for satirical newsletters and funny advice columns geared toward online observations and plenty of celebrity gossip. While it does take years of practice to become a comedic writer and stand-up comedian, there is always room for improvisation. While you may not be the next Jerry Seinfeld, you can very well become your own version of him or you.

One way to practice your humor chops is on your friends. Your friends will be the first to laugh at something funny you've said and the first to tell you if what your saying is actually offensive instead of clever. Trust me; it's better you rehearse for your friends than it is to go up on stage or at a party and get booed or, worse, silence. Another bit of advice is to be quiet—I know, weird, right? Trust me; it will serve you well to spend some time observing your friend group or the space around you. Listen to the conversations you regularly have.

Suppose you have a friend like Samantha, who I mentioned earlier. You can expect what she brings to the table, like relationship drama or stories from late-night expeditions that lead to her walking home the next morning with no shoes and even less pride. So, you can develop quippy remarks and clever comebacks for the subject matter she supplies. That's an example of constructed humor.

Part of being funny is the appropriateness of the situation; the last thing you want to be is obnoxious when trying to be funny. When poking fun at an individual or environment, make sure the tone meets the joke; this is called reading the room. Part of reading the room is seeing perspectives or, rather, other people's perspectives. Your material should fit the culture and social environment you find yourself in.

Comedy has long since been a vessel to address factual content while maintaining a nonjudgmental comedic connotation. This allows for bringing attention to the matter without overstepping personal opinion. In other words, you can talk about the Chinese culture and use fact-based observations without offending Chinese people with the content as long as it is done tastefully. It is especially important to understand where that line is located amongst the company you keep. Desensitization is a shift in the material that was once considered funny to what is now considered offensive. I repeat, the last thing you want to be known for as a comic is desensitization because once you've created this shift, it is extremely hard to be known as anything but someone who relies on comedic shock value.

When you add personalization to your humor, your jokes can take on politics, sexual tinge, and even educational themes. The idea is to develop your own personal view on any subject and use your standings on the topics as the framework for context based off personal experience. The "If it was me..." theory promotes a context that sounds like something that would actually happen to you. Therefore, making your story come to life and painting a mental picture of your involvement. Take Kevin Hart, for example.

We all know Kevin Hart from multiple stand-up specials, television, and film roles. He has a certain viewpoint and descriptive nature that is all his own. So, when he describes his childhood or his home life, you undoubtedly already have an idea of what it must be like to be Kevin Hart. So, while he tells his jokes or details a day in the life, you laugh because you can really see something like what he is describing happening to him. The amount of humility it takes to pull off the amount of "Kevin Hart Funny" takes guts and a grand acceptance of the "laugh at me" mentality.

While I thought the "laugh at me" mentality was a bad thing in my theater experience, I later found out it's actually more common than the "laugh with me" mentality; after all, the birth of comedy was meant to evoke laughter at oneself instead of others. In ancient Greek around the fourth century, comedy makes its grand appearance. While we typically think of jesters to the king or mimes, that is not where comedy began.

Aristotle began the classic conception of comedy. The primary focus of comedy was to bring light to certain social standings, follies, and politics. Aristotle is most known as being a 20-year apprentice of Plato and the man who rejected Plato's theory of forms. Aristotle was more than a mathematical and scientific genius; he was also an activist in a world where activists are killed for being open-minded or desiring change. So, he did what comics do today; he developed satire to address problems of injustice.

The word comedy is a derivation of the Greek verb meaning "to revel or reveal." Aristotle states that comedy originated in folksy songs and on stage in the form of improvisation. The idea was to hold a mirror up to society and reflect injustice and the nation's vices. The end result of this type of satirical purpose was that the follies and vices be mended without a direct prompt. Henri Bergson, a twentieth century French philosopher, shared his view of the corrective purpose of laughter; he said "Laughter is intended to bring the comic character back into conformity with society, whose logic and compliance to which the comic had previously abandoned." I'll reduce the Greek formalities by rewriting his words in English. "Laughter is a confrontation of one's own idiocy; shining a satirical spot on a man's shortcomings will make him aware of his mistakes and fix them." Basically, make fun of someone until they change the behavior that is being mocked, such as drinking too much, calling on prostitutes, or rolling in cow manure for fun. "My Strange Addiction" had to be around back then, wouldn't you think?

Long story short, philosophers had no business creating whatever version of comedy they thought that was. Leave it to the Greeks to make even the origin of comedy a tragedy too. But just as it reached its height in brilliantly sarcastic plays starring a dramatic comic by the name of Aristophanes, who developed what is now known as "old comedy," it was replaced by less vital and more imaginative comedy. The new comedy began around the mid fourth century; this type of comedic interpretation leaned away from critical comedy to what we now know as a romantic comedy or rom-com.

This brings us back around to the jester. You know the jester gets a bad rap; this medieval clown was as slapstick as they come and for a good reason. In the seventeenth century, France waged battles, kingdoms fell or had the threat of failing, and empires looked for a way to reduce the stresses of war; enter the jester. The only downfall to being a jester was a looming fear of beheading if said jester could not produce hearty laughter from its powerful counterparts. I mean, I'm reasonably funny, but would I be if my head depended on it? I doubt it. So, we all must give props to all the headless jesters who came before us.

Believe it or not, comedy wasn't always an endeared personality trait until around 1970. You can probably guess why comedy might not be the best quality to have in a world that suffered more than prospered. Unlike the kings and queens of the renaissance, we as a people didn't really feel like laughing during World War II or Vietnam. And that is the difference between monsters and morals.

Chapter 28: Get Your Banter On!

"I don't trust anyone who doesn't laugh."

— Maya Angelou

Banter is defined as an exchange of light, playful, teasing remarks, good-natured in tone. Banter is most commonly learned when growing up with siblings or close friends. Teasing is a great way to show off your playful side, and everyone loves entertaining back and forth humorous content. You might find that your funny small talk has an audience who can't help their curiosity. I realized in college that I was particularly good at unrehearsed humor; in fact, I was better at bantering than memorizing.

The ability to use your wit as a tool is priceless. Your wit determines how well you can come back after spoken to. Meaning after the person has spoken, you have one to three seconds to react, or else the point falls flat. If you don't have a quick wit, you can develop what I call "comeback collateral."

The idea of retaining comeback collateral is focused on the premeditated comeback. You can access any type of comeback there is in the world by doing a quick Google search titled "Quippy Comebacks." Try it. If you just searched for them, you would see that the resources for this topic are practically endless. What you need to do now is pick certain ones you may need in the future and memorize them. Think about it this way. You are at work, and your boss is bantering back and forth with another colleague about her taste in music, and she obliges him with quippy comebacks such as "Well, at least I listen to artists that are still alive!" and so on.

Knowing what kind of banter is needed is just as important as researching comebacks. You wouldn't want to overdo it or not do it at all, running the risk of seeming indifferent or boring. Just like the prior example, you want to avoid derogatory terms such as you're old or fat or lazy; the list goes on and on. What you might do is watch and listen for different ways your boss is interacted with, then form your own version of appropriate banter. Keep in mind the most likable behavior in recent office studies show the ability to banter is second only to politeness, on a scale of pleasantries in office environments.

If this skill doesn't come naturally and you find yourself freezing in your insecurities, here are some tried and true ways to regain your control over the playful conversation.

Find your tone: Once you have established a tone for your wit, practice it. Doing so will remove any chance of sounding rude or obnoxious; it is easy to fall prey to emotions you didn't even know you had. So, keep it light and airy, and you will laugh and make others laugh.

Be bold: Don't be afraid to shock and surprise; one of the rules of bantering is to quickly come back and strike when the iron is hot. Confidence is hard to ignore; use it when in playful discourse—it will be a huge leg to stand on. Show everyone you have an outgoing personality; this could actually help you get promoted and even invited to dinners.

Misinterpretation is gold: When I say misinterpretation in my lectures, I am met with confused faces. But the use of false impressions is quite effective, especially in a work environment. For example, a co-worker says "Hey, when Bob gets in, can you give him these papers?" You repeat back "When Bob gets in, shred these papers? Got it!" Pretending you heard them wrong is funny and shows your silly side as well.

Heritage comedy is the easiest comedy to achieve if you want to start simple. This type of satire is where a comic discusses humorous traits or stereotypes from their own culture or heritage. If you grew up in a funny family or under funny circumstances, this could be a valuable tool in social situations. It also allows for a bit of narrative comedy, which simply is a storytelling concept. Jeff Foxworthy is a great comedic example of heritage comedy. He grew up in the south with southern parents and in situations that are funny to just about everyone. Or Gabriel Iglesias; Gabriel tells a story of his growing up in a Mexican household complete with stereotypes and absolutely hilarious impersonations of his family members. I love to use this type of humor when telling stories of my weirdly funny background. It is the greatest example in my experience of historical laughter. If you have a funny story to tell, make sure you can tell it in a way that not only grabs your audience's attention but holds it until the very last punch line. The best advice I can give you is to practice your story, make plot points, and find your comedic cadence by saying the material aloud in the mirror or around nonjudgmental friends or family.

You don't have to attend an improv class to practice improvisation. I feel like a broken record sometimes when I say practice in the mirror, but practice in the mirror. As a matter of fact, practice everything in the mirror, from a clever wink to positive affirmations and self-talk. Find a way to know yourself in a deeper sense than you ever thought possible. Look yourself in the eyes, see who you are and what you aspire to be. The only way to become a memorable person is to be unforgettable, and that comes only after you find comfort in your own skin.

You can find all kinds of improv prompts online. Simply pick a scenario and play it out as your own. I will supply you with your first session here; take the prompt and finish it in the funniest way possible and don't you dare be afraid of looking silly! Go for it!

1. Excuse me, ma'am. I need to return these jeans for a refund. (Explain why)
2. Miss, I am afraid I did not order a hot dog for dinner. (Reorder your food)
3. Look, I know you hate this, but we need at least one good photo of you. (Act out avoidance)
4. Officer, please, no! Don't give me a speeding ticket! (Flirt or bargain)
5. Do you think Mother would like this crown or the silver one? (Describe a funny dad)
6. Sir, your suitcase will not fit in the overhead bin. (Try and fit it anyway)

7. Ladies and Gentlemen, please welcome today's guest—Pat Perkins—an expert on how to organize your desk! (Describe your version of the organization)

The idea behind improvisation is to show comedic range. If you can make organizing a desk funny, you are likely to make any common circumstance funny. It also allows for creating mannerisms that are all your own, along with gestures and tone of voice. Quick tip: once you have nailed down a specific kind of comedy, try and stick with it for a while so you can really capture the essence of that style before moving on. After all, what have I said about mastering a craft? You must practice and gain knowledge through experience. The same goes for being funny; if you don't know the ins and out of parody comedy, how will you know the limits of this style? I assure you; you don't want to find yourself on the wrong side of a parody.

A parody is the imitation of a group of people or a person. I parody my family all the time but let me tell you, before I got to this point, I suffered along with failed imitations of friends and colleagues that got me in trouble a few times. Some things to avoid when creating parodies:

1. If you think someone else's weight is funny, stop.
2. If you think someone else's race is funny, stop.
3. If you think someone else's handicap is funny, stop.
4. Death
5. Illnesses
6. Job loss
7. And even an ugly baby

I added the last one because I spent years trying to make the "ugly baby joke" a thing. Alas, no one wants to hear "Man, that's one ugg-o-ley baby!" It's considered rude and unhelpful; I know that now. It doesn't keep me from thinking it though, and that's keeping it real.

Chapter 29: Can Do Comedy – A Guide to Finding Your Kind of Funny

"Today you are you, that is truer than true. There is no one alive who is youer than you."

— **Dr. Seuss**

Comedy is the epitome of a happy ending. Comedy is not meant to be a vessel of anything other than laughter. The most common theme of satirical literature has always been a victory over unpleasant feelings or circumstances. When you go to a stand-up or Improv show, you go because you want to feel a type of joy that cannot be achieved in any other way besides laughter.

From Shakespeare's *A Midsummer Night's Dream* to Chris Rock's "Tamborine" special, the function remains the same—to bring amusement and happiness to the audience. Comedy, no matter the genre or style, has a profound impact on people's lives, allowing them to move ahead with cheer. But comedy is more than a great way to spend an evening, and humor is more than something to amuse.

Comedy and humor are interwoven into the very fabric of our human existence. It doesn't matter if you enjoy a good parody or dark humor told at funerals or even slapstick; comedy is everywhere. The question is, how does it pertain to you? Where do you fit in, in the world of making people laugh? The most basic form of human interaction is a connection; being able to connect on multiple levels is important. For instance, if you connect on an emotional level and a physical level but not on a comedic level, you may find your interactions lackluster when in conversations. A sense of humor isn't historically a requirement when considering a mate, but it should be. Imagine marrying someone who doesn't enjoy laughter; isn't that an important thing to know beforehand?

The importance of comedians and humor is more evident in the world today than it has ever been. If you are already charming, relatable, and self-assured, why not tackle this personality extra or add-on? While being funny can be inherited, it usually comes from personal experience and how you see the world. It helps to think of a personality as being four walls or four dimensions.

Chapter 30: The Personality Parrish

If You Want To Be Original, Be Ready To Be Copied

— Coco Chanel

1. Communication Trait: This is the ability to communicate confidently and effectively. This includes the capability to listen and the capacity to learn from mistakes or transgressions brought to your attention.

2. Emotional Capability: This is the ability to express your emotions in a healthy way, as well as understanding the emotions of others. Emotional intelligence is being able to balance compassion with kindness and empathy with mercy.

3. Adaptation Trait: This is the ability to understand your surroundings using critical thinking skills and when/how to apply them to appropriate situations. Approaching change courageously, granting enthusiastic opportunities to explore new possibilities with an open mind.

4. Interpreter Trait: This is the ability to adapt opinions and views and interpret different versions of the world as seen by others with the purpose of evidence, explanation, storytelling, or furthering education.

The fourth wall of the Personality Parrish is where comedy and cleverness meet. Understanding the perspective of an activist or political argument and being able to put it into your own words is the basis of comedic evolution.

On a scale of one to four walls, I would say humor would fall somewhere between the bathroom and your cement "rec room" also known as the place where your treadmill is rarely plugged in but always full of random clothing, and the place where you attempted a sit up or two last week. It is also the place where you occasionally park your vehicle.

One of the most common misconceptions surrounding the comedic world is: To be funny, you have to be original. This is not true, not even by a long shot. Every comedic actor, comedian, or even scriptwriters base their type of humor on one of the many different styles of humor. These styles have been around for centuries. At the same time, each individual has their own note-worthy contributions to the genre. They choose the idea behind the style that was created long before it existed. Here are some examples of comedy and some popular comics that execute them flawlessly.

Anecdotal: This style refers to the comedic detailing of personal stories that may be true or embellished for humorous effect. Think Sarah Silverman, George Lopez, and Patton Oswalt.

High Brow: This style is humor pertaining to cultural and sophisticated themes. Think Jimmy Kimmel and Jimmy Fallon—or any late-night comic.

Satirical: This style uses irony, mockery, and weaknesses in society. Think Robin Williams or George Carlin.

Screwball: This style uses wacky and absurd behavior by exaggerated characters in even more exaggerated scenarios. Think Jim Carrey, Will Ferrell, and Dave Chappelle.

Situational: This style is the basis for sitcoms and situation comedies or rom-coms. It draws humor from real-life scenarios and conversations. They can include other types of comedy, such as slapstick or screwball. Think Betty White, Bob Newhart, and Carol Burnett.

As you can see, all of the comics above have certain styles they thrive in. But this doesn't mean you have to fit inside any one box; it just means you have to find a box. In order to become the "funny one," there is only one requirement. That requirement is you have to be funny; not almost funny, actually funny. If you feel like the only thing keeping you from being clever, charismatic, and likable is your ability to make people laugh, then, by all means, boo-boo, find yourself a niche, and get to researching. There is a saying in the literary world "The more you read, the better your writing will be." If I didn't read, I would eventually run out of intelligent things to write about!

Chapter 31: Truth – "This may hurt a little."

"If you tell the truth, you don't have to remember anything."

— Mark Twain

The truth is, in most cases, black and white. If I told you an intentional lie, the reason behind that lie is intended deception. I want you to believe something about myself or a subject that is untrue. My sister does this nearly every time she meets someone new. She claims to be a "neat freak" and says she enjoys cleaning up her space because it makes her feel more in control of her day. The last time I ever saw her make a bed was in 1999 when she ran off and joined the United States Airforce.

I have always watched her relationships crash and burn like unmanned spaceships that have to abort their missions because of unforeseen issues. Unforeseen issues sum up every failed relationship attempt that involves "Candy Lies." I coined this phrase because of my sister, who always claimed "You have to sweeten them up with things they want to hear." I'll tell you the same thing I've been telling her for 20 years—if you have to lie at any point during a date, you are doing it wrong. Here's the thing; there are many different kinds of lies, all anticipating the same result to shield a truth. Here are some of the most common types of lying.

Lies of Deceit:

Most people use this attempt to con or escape the persecution of some kind.

Lies of Assurance:

This kind of lie comes in the form of promises that someone never planned on keeping. These lies can be labeled "Lies of Avoidance" and used to prolong something you know will eventually end, like a cheating spouse or partner.

Lies of Omission:

The act of omitting certain key truths that may be important or be deal-breakers.

Lies of Reconstruction:

This is what gossip produces; it allows for bits and pieces of the lie to distort the original context.

Lies of Exaggeration:

Or Candy Lies, this usually comes in the form of misrepresentation. If you tell someone you are a pro at sailing, then never want to go sailing, someone might begin to wonder if you know how to sail at all. Speaking in excess has never made anyone trustworthy because, like I have said before, if you have a talent to mention, make sure you can prove that talent.

My sister's long-standing issue with finding "Mr. Right" doesn't have much to do with the types of men she dates. It has everything to do with her exaggerated sense of self and refusal to cut this out of her profile. This is the end result of actually believing your own lies; she really thinks she is Martha Stewart. Fast forward to next week when Martha Stewart can be found running all over the place cleaning and sweating and folding—everything she claims to do on a daily basis—only to have "Mr. Right" open a closet door accidentally and finding himself knee-deep in my sister's poorly hidden trash.

The moral of the story is to avoid lying for no other purpose than to create a more entertaining version of yourself. Instead, *be* that version of yourself. Learn how to sail or clean and do it for you rather than for them. Because the lies we tell ourselves are the worst lies of all. How can you expect to grow if, instead of watering one personality, you choose to water two? One of the main focuses I have is for understanding different personality traits in this quest to become charismatic, clever, and likable. It is for you to formally examine and be in control of what energy you put off into the universe.

Lying and overestimating one's strengths is more like dark matter; it's unappealing and humiliating when people know you are doing it.

Part Five

There is no one formula that is more successful than others; that's why it's called a "game." Because no matter if you win or lose, everybody has fun, right? I would say it's called a game because, in the end, you must have losers and a winner who, for just a little while, feels on top of the world.

In the game of life, it is good to realize that you are, in some cases, not going to be the MVP. You are going to lose, and when you do, you are going to feel it. If that boy breaks your heart, you are going to feel immense pain. If your boss chooses another in that promotion, you are going to feel insecure. Understanding the concept of everything happens for a reason is not mandatory, but it is suggested. Being in control of every tear or pain and even your future can get heavy over time. Instead, try letting loose of the reins of life every once in a while, because the stark reality is none of us know what we are doing. The choice of being rain or a rainbow applies in even the simplest of terms when the star doesn't align; choose to be okay anyway.

My aunt Tracy swore by the Zodiac Calendar; she would exuberantly explain away your fear of commitment or your terrible taste in men by looking up your astrological sign. Horoscopes have long since been the go-to for understanding the reasons why people operate the way they do. My aunt whole heartily believed we were all made from stars and were sent here on our birthdays as gifts from another place. And that eventually, one day we will return to the stars; she didn't go into much detail about the mystery place or how to get back there. I assume this is because she didn't know or didn't get that far; she had a pretty serious drinking problem for most of my life.

Aunt Tracy may or may not have been under the influence when trying to explain how her horoscope is the one to blame after another failed relationship with a guy who drove a big truck, or lived in a big truck, I'm not completely sure of the dynamics between her and endless men by the name of Bubba; mom always told me to mind my own business, so I never really investigated. It was probably way out of my scale of relationship knowledge anyway.

Chapter 32: Are We Actually Made from Stars?

"We were written in the stars."

— Aisha Saeed

What do you think about my aunt's explanation of how we got here? I must admit I used to sit for hours listening to her and my mother share horoscopes and the mystery of death and life thereafter. I've never been scared of the unknown. I was always more analytical, I guess. Being an introspective child may have been more of an annoyance to the free-spirited conversational threads they weaved. I would often find myself absorbed in the wise speaking of my mom's best friend Tammy, who also believed her Leo nature is why she was so hard to love and the reason she couldn't go into the grocery store on the corner anymore. I will never forget my mother's response to hearing this nonsense "It's because you are a natural beast Tammy; you can't be fenced in!"

These are real people, folks; you can't make this stuff up. After Tammy grabbed a beer, they would all sit down with stones, cards, and candles and crank the tunes. Growing up, this was a weekly session; sometimes, I think my mom might have been a hippy or witch or astrologer—maybe she was all three? Whatever the case, maybe she was dedicated to learning about things so she could explain them to others. This is a trait that I inherited from my mother; she used to study the universe and practice her professor-like explanations on me. I couldn't have been a better student. I became distinguished in active listening by the time I reached middle school. This was partially due to my mother's pseudo lectures and her constant need for feedback to assure her I was listening and understanding the universe the way she taught it.

My therapist seems to think this was borderline child abuse, having me sit still for hours and comprehend the alignment of stars and galaxies and how they prove we don't belong here. But the truth, is I wouldn't change it for the world; because thanks to my intelligent mother, I too find learning impossible things mesmerizing. By the age of fifteen, I had already published several thesis papers on mind control and manifestation, many of which earned me scholarships and tuition assistance before any of my friends even thought of college.

Horoscopes, in many ways, do explain a lot of things, like natural disasters and holidays. They are thought to give insight into a person's future or unique characteristics. All this is gained from the relative positions of the stars and planets on the day or night you were born on. This astrological chart is, for some people, a guide through life, relationships, parenting, even death.

What does your astrological forecast say about you? I'll go first. My horoscope suggests that I am an Aries.

Aries: (March 21st to April 19th) Aries' element is fire, and zodiac symbol is the Ram. Aries are thought to be brave and have a tenacious ability to climb to the top of the mountain no matter what obstacles are thrown their way. This sign is warm and lovable but tends to draw attention to their unique ability to get in their own way. Literally and emotionally. The Aries can be loud, competitive, opinionated, and hard on themselves. But above all, the Aries can be terribly naïve to a fault.

Full disclosure: Every description of the Aries resonates with my personality on one level or another. My mother swore by this forecast, saying "This sign could rule the world if it just believed in itself a little more."

Taurus: (April 20th to May 20th) The Taurus's symbol is the Bull, and its element is Earth. This sign is known for its endless resilience and stubbornness. This sign is an anomaly, really; they tend to either be very accepting or extremely judgmental. They would prefer to be alone, but the fear of having no mate somehow makes them feel like an outcast. If you've ever met a Taurus, you would know they don't like being an outcast. Some not so likable traits would be laziness and over-indulgence. They are also comparable to an actual bull in that they can come off as frighteningly fierce when upset or serenely gentle.

Well, which one is it, fierce or gentle? This kind of question would undoubtedly get a book thrown at me 20 years ago.

Gemini: (May 21st to June 20th) Zodiac symbol for this water sign is the Twins. This is due to their unique ability to be incredibly versatile and neutral. They are also known as fast talkers; these people are able to, as my mother would say "Talk their way out of a wet paper sack." Meaning they could easily talk their way out of trouble. Geminis are clever by nature and make great communicators. The offhand is they can be self-absorbed and co-dependent. This sign can be quite the know-it-all. The only problem with that is most of the things they "know" are cliff notes of information. Frankly, because the actual paper or article bored them halfway through, so don't ask them to elaborate; they will attempt to confuse and quickly change the subject.

Cancer: (June 21st to July 22nd) This water sign gets the zodiac symbol of the Crab because they can be secretive and guarded. A hard enigma shell protects their emotional sensitivity, which can be dark and vast if damaged. Cancer signs have a great sense of self humor and love to be entertained. This sign loves hard and can be loyal to a fault. One of Cancer's worst qualities is holding grudges. I am fairly sure the one I was upset with 10 years ago still crosses my name off of invites in mutual situations. Like the Gemini, this sign tends to be codependent as well, especially to people they enjoy being around.

Leo: (July 23rd to Aug 22nd) The Leo's element is fire, and its symbol is the mighty Lion. Leos are known for being creative, passionate, and generous. They are also known for having an arrogant nature and plenty of self-centeredness. This sign is probably the biggest of them all because, like the lion, they prefer it that way. The Leo can be pleasantly shocking and fun to be around. People born under this sign usually have a flair for dramatics but are also natural-born leaders.

Virgo: (Aug 23rd to September 22nd) The Virgo's symbol is the virgin, with Earth being its element. Virgos are natural-born wallflowers. They are known for being introverts. They are highly intelligent and control freaks. They don't mind being introverts because, frankly, they don't think anyone is smarter or as capable as themselves. This sign loves to feel needed and appreciated. This is how they develop self-worth—by becoming part of something bigger than themselves. Think Silicon Valley; there are probably more Virgos than computers down there.

Libra: (Sept 23rd to Oct 22nd) The Libra's element is air, and the Scales are its symbol. Libras hate being alone; they are most often found in crowded bars on the weekend telling stories to drunk friends. Libras are not known to be in leadership positions due to the fact that they are notorious for their lack of decision-making skills. With that being said, they are, in fact, great self-starters and employable; mostly self-employable, seeing that they enjoy the freedom self-employment allows. Libras are classic perfectionists and enjoy being recognized for this trait. They make great interior designers with an adept ability to make any space super aesthetically pleasing.

Scorpio: (Oct 23rd to November 21st) The Scorpion is this sign's symbol, and water is its element. Like the scorpion, Scorpios are very guarded and will lash out if their space is invaded; they don't mind coming off as a mystery, they actually prefer it. While they aren't necessarily introverts, they are the ones standing back from the conversation just enough to observe the crowd. Scorpios always seem to have it all together and expect nothing less from friends and partners. This sign can be a great friend or mentor as long as you respect their intricate boundaries. They also make great dramatic actors because they can replicate certain darkness not reachable by any other sign.

Sagittarius: (Nov 22nd to Dec 21st) This fire sign is known as the Archer. This sign is opinionated and fierce if misunderstood or judged in any way. Emotion drives the Sagittarius, causing friction between friends and family, leading to trust issues and communication problems for this outgoing sign. While they are normally the loudest person at the party, they can also be the meanest by wielding truths or insults like a weapon. The Sagittarius can be found at gyms and whole food stores since they are obsessed with self-improvement.

Capricorn: (Dec 22nd to Jan 19th) Known as the Goat or the great Sea-goat, the Capricorn's element is surprisingly Earth. Capricorns are completely accepting of responsibility and capable of being responsible for many others. They are naturally paternal and able to suppress emotions to keep the peace. Meaning when they forgive, they literally forget. This sign doesn't require much attention and enjoys peace and quiet. Capricorns need to feel respected and useful; after all, they have been an adult since they could walk. If you are looking for a great friend, find a Capricorn.

Aquarius: (January 20th to Feb 18th) Aquarius's element is air, and its symbol is the Water Bearer. This sign doesn't do "feelings" and is known as the ultimate conspiracy theorist. The Aquarius is hard to convince otherwise after it has drawn its own conclusion. Meaning, talking them out of things or ideas is unlikely. This sign can be found in scientific labs and on location as news reporters. Their ability to turn off personal attachment is how they get through life. The Aquarius never seems quite like anyone else and longs for personal freedom. They are charming but hard to get to know on a relative basis.

Pisces: (Feb 19th to March 20th) The Pisces is a water sign, and their symbol is the Fishes. Like fish, the Pisces wish for no boundaries. They want to swim the entire ocean away from society, in endless quiet. This sign is the "insecure" sign; they are sensitive and have a fear of being judged or, worse, ignored. Irrelevance is Pisces' worst nightmare. Pisces can come off as boring but have a treasure trove of creativity they tend to keep to themselves. They are painters or artists but rarely make a living doing this. Pisces are often therapists or accountants. They love to help everyone but themselves.

Astrological signs are technically a conspiracy theory, adapted by society over many generations as fact or proven science. The hard reality is it's nothing more than celestial navigation with the intent of foretelling destinies. Come along while we take a step back in time to when horoscopes and signs really started to take hold of our species.

Chapter 33: Horoscope History 101

"I don't believe in astrology; I'm a Sagittarius and we're skeptical."

— Arthur C. Clarke

In the early seventeenth century, the world was full of chaos and power struggles, leading to violence and famine. Revolutions raged, and slave trades were in full swing, causing an extremely dark outlook on the meaning of life. Children were being kidnapped, and mothers were being murdered and mutilated for sport in some cases. During times of war and injustice, the human brain grasps at straws finding anything to make it all sensical.

Enter Galileo, a famous astronomer who connected most of the astrological dots during his career and telescope discoveries. He is most known for discovering the moons of Jupiter and some other cool science things. But he also changed our view of the universe by making it less scary and more of a religious experience.

In Galileo's day, the study of astronomy was only used for calendars. It is widely believed that it was his astronomy students, not some otherworldly creature or star men, who actually produced the horoscopes we know today.

Some of you will not like the scientific skepticism attached to star-born selection. But the ugly truth is it's unreliable; some people can't find themselves inside any of these signs. If you really take a look within yourself, you can pick out some relatable traits, of course, but most of these signs are quite similar and vague. I mean, yeah, I am intelligent and sometimes a pushover but is that really something given to me by a constellation above my mother's hospital bed the very minute I was born? What about the constellation above my mother's bed when I was conceived? Why doesn't that count as well? Technically I was brought into the world on that very night, or at the very least, my essence was. But before we get into a pro-life situation, I may never find myself out of, let me be clear. If horoscopes are to be believed, then it helps to understand how they believe we got here. Astronomical enthusiasts believe we are made from stars; they just don't exactly narrow the idea down to specific creation dates.

Most theology concepts begin with conception; this is why Christians believe in pro-life. I get it—to each his own; but if your horoscope doesn't start until the day you were born, then Christians who practice horoscopes are living on two sides of the fence, wouldn't you think? So, with that in mind, wouldn't my astrological sign begin the night I was conceived?

If my theory is allowed for consideration, that will turn me from an Aries into a Cancer, and I couldn't be more opposite from a Cancer. As a matter of fact, I have the tendency to make quick enemies of Cancers. My best friend in high school was a Cancer and the only Cancer I have ever been friends with for an extended amount of time. My mother's explanation for this is opposites attract, and my shy, crabby friend was dependent on my ram-like strength and quirky nature. It was meant to enhance the Crab's sociability and to test my Aries patience and ability to understand emotions more clearly.

Her theory makes a lot of sense. But thanks to my need to understand, well maybe not understand, but make sense of what I am being exposed to, I dig; and through such digging, I can arrange my own thoughts and make it all make sense in one form or another. My mother's insistence on my learning the inner workings of the universe eventually backfired when I jokingly suggested all her knowledge was, in fact, bologna. In turn, she stopped asking me to sit and took her thoughts elsewhere. I would guess to a simpler audience.

I am aware it is not my job to discredit horoscopes; it is my job, however, to explain what they are intended for and why everyone is so drawn to celestial compatibility and human nature. I believe if it weren't for stars, we wouldn't have poets, and love depends on poets.

Might I suggest instead of finding a horoscope that fits your personality, I ask you to defy your given horoscope? Yes, you read that right. If you happen to be a Scorpio, your sign pretty much lives in a state of avoidance. This leaves you no other option but to get up and get out there. Hiding behind a belief system that you are incapable of changing is about the most ignorant thing a human being can do. Since the zodiac system has been a part of human life for so long, we have unintentionally become contingent on this imposed reality.

Take, for example, my sign. I am thought to be highly intelligent, creative, and impulsive. My impetus-driven sign is most known for ADHD. While I may be both of those things, so is a Leo, and the opposite of which would be a Pisces. What would happen if I took some of my personality from each sign? You would get a sign that was not only smart but intuitive. I would become subtle and strong, having an ingrained balance of social and individual success that garnered respect, not just for my ability to be very well put together but also my instinctive ability to stay quiet when needed. The end result would be the obvious transformation into a superhuman.

Don't believe me? I challenge you to do the same. Instead of being, say, a Taurus full-time, allow yourself to employ one sign that is similar to yours, then flip it on its ear and apply one sign that you are least compatible with. Pull positive traits from both and practice their strengths. Eventually, the strengths you have now will become entwined with strengths you have gained from your new sign mates.

This goes along with the process of becoming intelligent; to become superiorly smarter than your peers, you must absorb their knowledge, which means constantly learning from everything and everyone around you. This involves studying everything you are told, discover, or experience, and so on. If you agree to become a sponge of your environment, you will become an expert in that habitat. So, if your end game is to become a charismatic, clever, and likable person, you have to harness the capability to adapt to the climate around you. When you do, you can harness the skills to create something I like to call the "Me Show." A show where everyone seems to want to tune in and be entertained daily. So, stay tuned for the chance to become everyone's favorite sitcom star.

Chapter 34: Welcome to the "Me Show"

"When I do stand-up, I'm basically doing a one-man show."

Chris Rock

If this idea sounds conceited or self-absorbed, it's because you may not be comfortable with being the center of attention. But the book you are reading is about self-discovery; you are trying to become the center of attention essentially. For one reason or the other, you find yourself more like furniture than works of art in social situations, correct?

There are a number of ways to produce your version of a one-man show. There's the "Whiney Girl" show, the "Masculine Man" show, and even the "A Series of Unfortunate Events" show. But those don't show what people want to see or hear about; the shows they want to see are ones that have the ability to escape life for a moment.

If you want to captivate an audience, you must bring a particular insight, one that will draw them into a world you've created just for the night. This is not an essay on becoming a good liar; it's about becoming a good storyteller. After all, you wouldn't call J. K. Rowling a liar, would you? Harry Potter is a fictional character, and none of that magic is based on real-life, but try telling that to my 10-year-old niece who asked for the "real Harry Potter wand" for Christmas and received the best version of a fake wand I could find. I'm sure she didn't appreciate my arrogance and horrible reciting of one of Potter's famous spells, but that's neither here nor there.

If you are a natural storyteller, you will find this step extremely easy; if not, don't worry about it. This, like everything, is attainable by a certain amount of practice. Begin by finding one area in your life that is interesting, funny, or provocative and start enhancing it with a storyline. Here's an example.

Last week I was in the grocery store, and due to not paying enough attention, I walked right into a new promotional stand that housed thousands of tiny oranges. The oranges went sliding every which way across the floor; then a supermarket employee asked me what had happened, and I told her I had not a clue. In saying that, I suggested there may or may not have been a ghost in the store and that they should call a priest or psychic or whatever and kept moving. During the time that it took me to reach the cash register, the young employee decided to check the cameras for this spiritual activity I previously spoke of. The employee surprised me when she tapped me on the shoulder as I was leaving the store. My first thought was "Did I forget to pay for the things under my cart?" Followed by "What is going on?" To which she replied with "I can see you, and I can touch you." Confused, I asked her "Are you okay?" completely forgetting I had just spoken to her. Her response was "If you are a ghost, which you have to be because it was clearly you who knocked over the oranges, why choose me to reveal yourself to? Is it because I can see dead people?"

If I were a better person, I might have told her I wasn't a ghost or the truth; I was just so embarrassed by my goof that I made it up. How could I have predicted that my silly excuse would lead this abstract woman on a quest to find Casper? Instead, I assured her she could talk to the other side and that she should probably tell the world of her new spiritual connection, maybe even start her own Medium service to help others. And hit her with a booming "Boo" on my way out the door. I don't know where that young lady ended up, but I hope it wasn't in prison for spiritual fraudulence. You see, when it comes to being the bigger person, I would rather be the smartest person, and that is a day in the life of Mrs. Mayhem—cue the laughter, cue the interest. See? Easy.

The only thing missing from this little gem of a plot is the way I illuminate it with my voice. The mannerisms and crispness that make up my insatiable wit and ability to draw a crowd are missing here. When telling this story aloud, make sure to add a sense of willing ambivalence to my continued shopping and a couple of different speaking voices, using all of this to create a movie-like scenario.

There is one thing that everyone wants and loves to do while having a good time, and that is to laugh. If you can garnish even a small amount of wittiness and banter, you can make people laugh. While I might be outgoing enough to star in my own show, some may be just outgoing enough to become a co-star in someone else's show. This is, in its own way, the same as having your own show without the pressure of hitting every mark.

My brother has been the co-star in my show since birth. He is four years younger and was my biggest playmate growing up.

My sister was only 19 months older than me but always seemed to have her own friends and a general distaste for my being alive. So, she didn't make a good go-to for play, obviously. My brother never really had a choice in my presence but also didn't want to throw himself off a metaphorical bridge every time I came near him. A win is a win in these types of situations.

Anyway, my brother was my audience, my laugh machine, and my biggest comedic critic. I respected my brother's opinion and learned from his comedic timing through our days role-playing as stand-up comedians and funny movie scripts we wrote as a team. Even now that we are older and have children and lives of our own, you can see the dynamic between us is always funny. When we are together, we play off each other's stories like improv students play off words. He has the ability to add so much fun energy to my stories. At the same time, I add witty banter and comebacks to his stories as I have already heard them before. The fact is his role in my comedy was the very role he was meant to play. When we aren't around each other, my brother goes back to the serious, sometimes witty person he is, and I remain the star of my show.

If you wish to become the person everyone calls or goes to for a good time, you have to become the star. But if you are a person who doesn't think mass storytelling is your thing but finds peace in laughter, you can become the co-star and be your kind of funny. If the whole world was made up of people like me, parties would be nothing but competitions between main characters. And everyone knows a good movie consists of supporting actors; the main character would never accomplish anything if it weren't for the help of the supporting cast.

If you find yourself in the background or as an extra, try to imagine yourself as the main character; because the reality is, the main character is normally the outgoing one. If you just can't be as outgoing as the main event, don't stray away from the lead actor's spotlight; find a way to stand in it, or like my brother, make it shine brighter. Because if a movie or television show wins an award, everyone involved in that show's success rushes that stage, right?

Do you remember when I suggested that if you can't find a light, then be one? The same goes for entertainers; if you find yourself at a party that seems to be lacking the main character or focus in general, become it. Get out there and test your improv; see how well you can put what you've learned into a real situation.

The quickest way to master a craft is to study it; ask any theatre "understudy" what they do as "understudies." They will tell you they watch, listen, and learn from whomever it is they may have a chance of becoming. In the world of theatre, there must always be an understudy for the main and sometimes costars. This is the reasoning behind the old saying "The show must go on!" This statement is not dependent on the main character's ability to show out. It is based on the ability to show up. In some cases, the first choice isn't the one that graces the stage due to, say, an accident or sickness. But the show must go on so, cue the understudy. In some of the most amazing theatrical stories, the understudy had to go on for the star and ultimately became the star because the understudy practiced and observed the first choice in every way possible; becoming so much like the star it was hard to tell them apart.

You see, it's not really about what content you create for these performances; it's how well you can orchestrate them. This leads me to my next step.

There is one truth of life every human on earth will encounter; that truth is everyone has a carnal need to understand. We need to understand who we are, where we came from, even what our world consists of. Knowledge is the beginning and end of everything. With that said, there is absolutely no excuse for "winging it." Imagine if Tesla was like "Don't worry, Edison! I'm just going to wing this alternating current thing." Famous words you wish were spoken—but scientific equations and such, am I right?

Chapter 35: Social Media Stand-Off

"It takes discipline not to let social media steal your time."

Alexis Ohanian

Hopping on the bandwagon is an understatement when it comes to the rise in social media platforms. Honestly, I never expected Facebook to become a permanent construct in the lives of everyone I know. I definitely never expected to have to compete with a computer in every aspect of my life. When the very first feed went out, we lost our sense of communication entirely.

The ugly truth is social media isn't ruining lives; that's not what it was invented for. But rather, your relationship with it and how you consume it is. The beauty of sites like Instagram and Twitter is you can be anyone you want to be. The ability to crop photos and use filters has created a network full of fake impressions and imaginary lives. This causes others to, you guessed it, become envious and self-conscious and frankly distressed over what they can contribute to the masses.

If your life revolves around what other people are doing instead of what you should be doing, chances are you have an addiction to social media. There should never come a time where you ignore what you need to do because you are watching others do whatever it is they're doing. Your screen time should never be longer than one hour. I know it sounds impossible, but I assure you it is possible.

Here are some ways social media apps are micromanaging your life:

1. You give most of your time to others: What I mean by that is when you find yourself with a bit of free time, you choose to open your Facebook app and begin scrolling. Or when your children want to play or be noticed, you shoo them away because you're "busy"; the same goes for your significant other. The solution is turning off the screen and refocusing on real life.

2. Irrelevant information is bad for your brain: When your eyes and ears become virtual, you open the door for mind-numbing experiences. A little-known fact is the enemy of intelligence is factless information. I can't tell you how many times I've seen the term "fake news" or someone giving their opinion on something they clearly have no education on. There is nothing worse than giving power to irrelevant information or pseudo-intellectuals.

3. Happiness is the absence of Envy: Social media has become a tool for showing you all the things you should have. Like I mentioned before, if you have an already deflated image of yourself due to lower self-esteem or the presence of jealousy, social media could really be harmful to you. That screen could be the reason you feel uninspired or depressed. When you compare your life to others, you will never see the true value of your accomplishments.

4. Your life becomes entertainment for others: Good or bad, every day, your life becomes a status update or a meme. And every time you post something negative or uncomfortable the whole world sees; it's like opening your front door and letting everyone see inside your house. The word personal seems to have lost its importance these days. Personal space has now become a universal space; protect your individuality from judgments by shutting your front door. Keep in mind that a Facebook friend is not a real friend, most people who follow you do not wish you well, and every sad status about how you "just can't deal" is like a vast movie marquee of self-defamation. Trust me, all of those people have front-row tickets to your demise. Don't give anyone that power!

If you connected with even one of these scenarios, I would suggest the 7-day Digital Detox Challenge. This is a challenge I promise will change your life. If there is one takeaway from this book, I hope this is it; because to be a better person, you must challenge every aspect of your life, including the way you are perceived online.

Chapter 36: 7-Day Digital Detox Challenge

"Distracted from distraction by distraction"

— T.S. Eliot

Day 1: Download the phone usage app and set the limit to two hours a day.

If you've never heard of a usage app, don't fret. It is super easy to install. Just type it in your app store and download it. This app is simply a tool to gauge how much time you spend on your phone and gives you the ability to set the alarm for excess usage.

Day 2: Leave your phone when you go out walking or while eating dinner.

Giving your attention to things like self-care or conversations will allow for taking in your surroundings and enjoying dinner without having to take a photo of what you're eating or doing (i.e., irrelevant information).

Day 3: Don't take your phone out at social gatherings.

Same concept. Avoid detracting from face-to-face encounters. Having a phone in your hand can cause you to become withdrawn and eliminate eye contact. Two things that will destroy human interaction and make you look uninteresting and vague. It also lessens something called "The Google Effect." It's the constant need to know the answer to every question; this is common in social gatherings.

Day 4: Don't use your phone after 9 pm.

Take the time you would usually catch up on news feeds and pamper yourself instead. You've spent all day working after work. Take an hour to catch up, comment, and observe. After that, put your cell on the charger and refocus your attention on taking a hot bath or getting a workout in, or even making dinner. There is no wrong way to practice self-care, and remember, social media addiction is the opposite of self-care.

Day 5: Turn off notifications.

Not only are these little insights annoying, but they take away your focus. I have fallen victim to the incessant beeps myself. I'll be making dinner or cleaning the house and hear "ding-ding," causing my attention to be drawn to what I'm missing, and so I grab my phone and begin answering emails or texts. Before I know it, I have been cruising Instagram for three hours, unable to remember how I got there. So, set those pesky buzzes to silent and continue on about your day.

Day 6: Don't use your phone while you are alone.

This has to be the hardest of all the steps. Because, like most people, social media is entertainment. When you become bored or lonely, you pick an app and tune in. It's like television; there is always something on. And why on earth would you rather stare at a wall when you can be visually stimulated? The answer is you don't always have to be stimulated. I know that seems crazy, but it's true. Choose to allow the beauty in the world to invigorate your senses. Grow a garden, paint a canvas, or even walk your dog instead of watching other people do so. I promise you it will make you feel better; give it a shot.

Day 7: Don't charge your phone for a few days.

At this point, you probably think I'm just mean. On the contrary, I am optimistic that by day seven, you have allowed for less screen time, making it easy to tackle this task. On Friday afternoon, when your phone tells you it needs a charge, take the charger and phone and place them out of sight. Leave the phone uncharged until Sunday night, when you will plug it in and head to bed. Monday morning, your phone will be charged and ready to go. This doesn't mean first things first check your notifications; it means it is ready to be used responsibly. In rehab, the therapist doesn't tell drug addicts that the "need" to use isn't real because it is. The need to get that fix will only fade away if you ignore it completely over time. Recovering isn't easy; it can sometimes feel like a fight to the death. Relapse is common in addiction and know that you will at some point relapse. But recovery is constant, and you will have to remind yourself of the reason you are doing it.

After the first seven days, I challenge you to a full digital detox—seven days without social media of any kind. This means removing social media apps completely from your device and using your phone only for emails and call connections. If you can complete the last seven days of the challenge, you will never look at social media the same again. Finding out how much time you devote to irrelevant things will shock you and hopefully prompt you to make a mindful change in your digital footprint.

Social media, while it often feels like you need it, isn't a basic human need. I have never once seen Facebook hug anyone or save anyone from a burning building. Think about that when investing so much time into something that obviously doesn't love you back.

Epilogue

Loving who you are shouldn't be a challenge if you use what you've learned in this book. The only thing preventing self-love is self-loathing. This quality can be caused by others or developed over time and even through failed attempts to change. Nevertheless, you weren't born appalled by who you are; experiences and bad choices along with emotional trauma inflicted through no fault of your own has led you here.

The resounding truth about the human experience is that we cannot be found in the past or the future; we can only be found in the here and now. But by honoring our psychological and evolutionary needs, we create a greater understanding of why they are important and necessary for the human experience. Let's face it, yes, you have a personal history, aspirations, and goals. You also have a name, a persona, and a moral ground. But there is so much more to you than what you allow the world to see.

I do not claim to be a character guru, but I do know a thing or two about self-condemnation. The reason I got into the self-help industry is that I have had to pull myself up by my bootstraps more times than I can count. I've been on the losing end of life far more than I have been on the winning side. The only difference between someone who hates themself and someone who loves themself is the ability to understand who and why they are.

People that tend to give up are less likely to accept the person they are. The reason is quite simple; giving up and giving in is a lot easier than working through and executing change. Giving up is never an option when it comes to self-help; it's right there in the name, to help oneself. By doing so, you are allowing your inner critic the fuel needed to reiterate how big of a failure you are. I haven't met one person who has attended my lectures that claimed they didn't need to change.

Inability to change makes you powerless against your demons. Those pointy-tailed jerks feed off your disappointments and "mess-ups." Stop feeding the monkey on your back, and it will be forced to move on to a new food source, or with any luck, disappear completely. Nothing is more sinister than sleeping with the devil because the true root of evil when referring to self-nourishment is allowing invisible captures to deprive you of living your life.

Trauma, anxiety, depression, bipolar, PTSD, and other mental states are responsible for reducing self-love because they are thought to be problematic and overwhelming disorders, and that couldn't be further from the truth. As someone who suffers from ADHD, I have lived most of my life in survival mode. This wasn't a mode where I allowed myself to be in friendships or relationships until way into my twenties. The reason behind that type of essential introverted behavior was self-preservation. I was always concerned with what would be said of me behind my back. That type of insecurity led to too many years standing on the sidelines, watching the people around me enjoy life and eventually leaving me behind.

When I realized my true existence, it wasn't a coming-of-age situation or a melodrama starring the sassy best friend who helps me find a lover, but instead, I found myself. Of course, there will be plenty of credit given to my helpers and mentors along the way, but in the end, I am the one who saved my life. It took years and a lot of courage to climb mountains of doubt and reach the other side.

It sounds cliché, but one day I just got sick of making excuses for myself and decided to try something different, because what I was doing clearly wasn't working and wasn't going to work in the future. So, I started to research information about healing childhood trauma and self-inflicted mental trauma. And the results were less informative than what I had hoped for. But this didn't deter me from heading to the local bookstore, where I sat for several hours reading self-help books about every topic I needed to know about. There were books about ADHD and depression and the correlation between the two disorders, as well as coping skills for anxiety and other forms of self-soothing. Immediately I felt calmer and less like a feather in the wind. I returned to that bookstore so many times I was offered a job there. Naturally, I had to decline the offer due to my other jobs and heavy workload, but the offer was exciting to me.

The offer meant more than what the owner thought it could; it gave me a sense of wonder. I wondered if I was as unapproachable as I had previously thought. I also wondered if I thought I was unworthy of maintaining friendships all of these years or if I was told that at one point or another. The thought resonated in me and led me to books on emotional trauma and abuse. I read something one day while sitting on the floor of that dusty bookstore. "Don't let pain define you; let it refine you."

Tim Fargo is an amazing life coach and a brilliant writer, and one of the reasons I accepted the ultimate truth of our existence. The mind is a terribly long and intricate corn maze you didn't ask to be lost in. Everyone has this maze, but not everyone has self-realization. As long as you remain comfortable in confusion, you will continue to go around and around in a circle of perpetual ignorance. Have you ever heard the saying "Ignorance is bliss"? If you haven't, allow me to break it down. Being ignorant is a choice, a choice someone makes when they are too lazy to find the answer. Instead of learning about politics or the way the world operates, most people choose to remain in a state of stupidity.

Learning isn't a point in time; there is no cut-off date to knowledge. There are two types of people in this world. The people who find peace in knowing and the people who find ways to avoid it. When you graduated high school, what was your first thought? Was it the thought of being free from learning or excitement for furthering your education? If it was the latter, congratulations, you are part of an elite group of individuals and are probably making adequate contributions to society. If you didn't want to continue with your education, there is no shame or loss of respect but a chance to discover a side of yourself that has always wanted to learn.

The human mind demands and deserves the chance to learn. It doesn't really matter what you learn. In theory, it's unquestionably about the continuance of positive behavior. If you train your mind to accept what makes you different, you can continue with a behavior that is beneficial to creating a more positive state of mind, in turn creating a more positive life. The damage that occurs when the option of self-preservation is taken away is not just substantial; it is dangerous.

In my classes, I always leave my audience with positive affirmations. This prompts them to see their world differently; by attending my lecture, they have already decided a change is necessary. And many of them stay after to ask further questions about the road to recovery. One question I have heard more than any is "What happens if none of this works for me?" And that is a solid question, one I am sure most people have. And my answer to that question is this "What if it does? Who will you be at the end of this process?" Preservation is far more powerful than any personality flaw you may have; doubt leaves room for conviction, and we all know the end result of disbelief, giving up. Make conscious decisions to evade reluctance and remain full speed ahead when tackling self-realization and self-care.

Whether you believe in the fault in our stars or the power of positivity, do so in such a way that even Bill Nye himself couldn't disprove your theory. The way you feel about yourself isn't up for debate or open to suggestions anymore past today. Be situated in your life to the degree that baffles other human beings; meaning have such a great outlook on life that it inspires others. The only barrier between who you are and what people think of you is perspective. Simply put, you can do everything in your power to change and evolve, even learn how to fight for yourself. But what you can never do is change someone else; it's just not a thing.

Change is good for everyone, but not everyone wants to change. You can become charismatic, clever, and likable all you want, but it won't change someone's opinion of you.

Learning to accept the haunting truth of not being liked is almost impossible to do. Human nature thirsts for acceptance and likability more than it thirsts for water. Being everyone's favorite person is impossible. The key to happiness doesn't open that door. But the door it does open is the door to your own heart.

I wish nothing more for you but a long, happy life full of interesting people and even more interesting conversations.

I will leave you the same way I leave all my speaking engagements: with positive affirmations to help you along the way. Additionally, be thankful and aware of the people who are sent to help you and protect you. Learn everything you can and apply that knowledge in every aspect of this confusing, wonderful, and exceptional life we have the pleasure of living.

CPSIA information can be obtained
at www.ICGtesting.com
Printed in the USA
BVHW061239200223
658846BV00015B/359